CU00663260

Prais

You Ar(

'This is a wonderful companion for Lent by David Walker. It is short but deep, and engages the reader in both prayer and reflection. A perfect way to explore what it means for all of us to belong to Christ in a challenging world.'

Justin Welby, Archbishop of Canterbury

'I have a great admiration and respect for David Walker. It was so good to read these revealing reflections on the scriptures which he offers in the light of his experience. They are highly accessible while being theologically profound. I hope others will find them as illuminating and inspiring as I did.'

John Inge, Bishop of Worcester

'Using Lenten scriptural readings and rooted in his own personal journey, David Walker helps us to recognise the presence and activity of God in our own life, and as a consequence our connectedness and belonging to all God's creation. This is down-to-earth, sound biblical and pastoral theology, as you would expect from Bishop David.'

Brother Benedict, Provincial Minister, The Society of St Francis

'In these thoughtful, touching and often candid reflections, David Walker reveals how he learned that we belong to God through other people. In his father, teachers, therapist, wife, parishioners, children and grandchildren, God becomes vividly present to him through fierce love, inspiring intellect, warm hospitality, quiet wisdom – and even the hatred of a suicide bomber's attack on the city where Walker is much-loved bishop.'

Paul Vallely, author of *Pope Francis: Untying the knots – the struggle for the soul of Catholicism*

'In this remarkable collection of devotions, David Walker combines deeply personal reflections with refreshingly practical observations on the Christian life. The message is humble and clear: in our Lenten battles for our better selves, we belong to God and to one another. This is writing as liberating as it is demanding – full of challenge, comfort and quiet joy.'

Loretta Minghella, First Church Estates Commissioner

The Bible Reading Fellowship
15 The Chambers, Vineyard
Abingdon OX14 3FE
brf.org.uk

The Bible Reading Fellowship (BRF) is a Registered Charity (233280)

ISBN 978 0 85746 758 4
First published 2019
10 9 8 7 6 5 4 3 2 1 0

Acknowledgements
Scripture quotations are taken from The New Revised Standard Version of the
Bible, Anglicised edition, copyright © 1989, 1995 by the Division of Christian
Education of the National Council of the Churches of Christ in the United States of
America. Used by permission. All rights reserved.

Every effort has been made to trace and contact copyright owners for material
used in this resource. We apologise for any inadvertent omissions or errors, and
would ask those concerned to contact us so that full acknowledgement can be
made in the future.

A catalogue record for this book is available from the British Library

Printed and bound by CPI Group (UK) Ltd, Croydon CR0 4YY.

You Are Mine

Daily Bible readings
from Ash Wednesday to Easter Day

DAVID WALKER

To Sue,
who has journeyed with me over so many years.

Contents

Introduction

In search of belonging

Welcome to this series of daily reflections for Lent. Over a number of years I have been exploring the notion of what Christian belonging means. How do we belong with God and with Jesus? And how do our human lives help or hinder us along the way?

I took up the issue because I felt it was very much underplayed. I could find lots of writing about what Christians believe and no end of (often conflicting) viewpoints on how we should behave. But all of this felt to be missing the central point. Above all, we are called, as the ancient Israelites were called long ago, to be the people of God. Before anything else our relationship is one of belonging. And that cannot just be collapsed into a combination of the things we believe and the moral standards we subscribe to.

Along the way, I discovered four dimensions to human belonging that together seemed to me to make up a reasonably complete model. I studied them initially through a sabbatical, which then turned into a series of academic papers published in various journals, and on into the work that brought me my doctorate in 2014.

We belong, whether with God or elsewhere, through a combination of these four elements.

Activities are the things we do sufficiently often to have a sense of commitment that goes beyond the current instance. In Christian circles they might include attending services regularly, a routine of personal prayer and Bible study, being part of a fellowship group or serving on a church council. *Events* are the big 'one-off' things that we do, whether family celebrations, community events or the major feasts of the Christian calendar. Alongside these, I found that we belong through our relationships with *People* and with specific *Places*. All of these can be means by which our sense of belonging with God is sustained and grown. If you are interested in the model in more detail, or in how it can be turned to practical use for a church that wants to reach out in mission, you will find lots more about it in my book *God's Belongers* (BRF, 2017). It's deliberately written not to require any of the detailed statistical analysis from the earlier academic work.

In working towards both my PhD and the later book, I was struck by how readily a model developed to understand Christian belonging in the 21st century mapped on to the stories of the Bible. Indeed, the biblical material seems to me to show a better balance between the four dimensions than many churches achieve today. So I was delighted to be invited by BRF to approach the same issue, of what it means to belong with God, from the perspective of daily devotional reflections. This current book is the fruit of that work.

Much of what I write is rooted in my own personal journey with Christ, over the 40-plus years since my faith came alive as I was preparing to go to university. I probably reveal more about my own faith and challenges here than in anything I have ever previously written. I hope that you find this personal dimension helpful. It is certainly not meant to be self-indulgent in any way, but to build on the one thing that I really know and know well: what it has meant to seek to belong with God as Father, and with Jesus Christ, over the course of a life lived predominantly in public Christian ministry.

For each week of Lent the reflections will follow a particular theme within belonging. We will begin with ten days exploring how we belong directly with God the Father and with Jesus Christ. Over successive weeks we will turn our attention to how we belong with the people who are closest to us; with the great figures of the Bible and Christian faith; with the wider community and its special places; and with the big celebrations and events of the Christian cycle and human life. Between them these will pick up the different dimensions of belonging set out above.

This pattern will be slightly interrupted for the Sunday reflections from the second to fifth Sundays in Lent. Rather than the weekly themes, these will follow the principal gospel reading that is used on those days in many churches across a wide range of denominations. This year they are focused on a series of encounters between Jesus and particular individuals, as set out in John's gospel. Each of them has something to say to us about how we belong with and through Christ. Finally, for Holy Week we shall follow Jesus on the journey from Palm Sunday to Easter Day, discovering how to belong more closely with him on each stage of his passion and resurrection.

At times I have found writing these reflections deeply moving. I have discovered the mark of God in my life in places where previously I had not been aware of the strength of that presence. At one point I was drawn to describe the exercise of producing daily reflections as like writing a series of love letters to God. Again and again, as I have sought to look into both the scriptures and my own life, I have heard in the silence the one who assures me, ever more strongly, 'You are mine.' My hope and prayer is that you who read it will hear something of the same, not because I am saying it to you but because one who is far greater is able to speak to you through the words I have been given.

May God bless you in your Lenten discipline and give you joy and courage to complete your course. And may you ever hear him whisper those precious words of belonging in your ear: 'You are mine.'

Ash Wednesday to the end of Week 1

BELONGING WITH THE FATHER AND THE SON

To be a Christian is to find one's primary belonging in a relationship with God through Jesus Christ. Every other belonging is subordinate to and consequent upon that. Even our most precious and intimate human relationships cannot compare with what it means to belong with one who knows us completely and utterly and, notwithstanding that, loves us more deeply and eternally than any other could.

For that reason, for the first ten days of Lent, from Ash Wednesday until the Saturday before the second Sunday, these daily reflections focus on different aspects of what it means, and how it feels, to belong with the Father and with his Son Jesus Christ. We will meet the one who feeds us, teaches us, forgives us and heals us. We will engage with the creator, who is also the one who conquers evil and calls us to eternity. And we will join Jesus in his fasting and temptation.

Ash Wednesday

Beginning our discipline

And the Spirit immediately drove him out into the wilderness. He was in the wilderness for forty days, tempted by Satan; and he was with the wild beasts; and the angels waited on him.

MARK 1:12–13

Over recent years I've become more and more aware that my relationship with God is not simply mediated through my mind and intellect but through every part of my body and each of my senses. I've discovered how the posture I adopt for praying can make a real difference, whether raising my arms towards heaven or sitting cross-legged on the floor. And I've learned to make more of icons or holy pictures as well as songs and music, in order to focus my prayer in particular directions. Touch and taste and smell have also become more important components of my spirituality. I might pray while gripping a cross or slowly eating a piece of chocolate.

Today we begin the season of Lent. I expect many of us have already made a decision about some discipline we intend to follow over these next weeks. I hope that the rhythm of reading the daily passages in this book, and setting aside time to reflect on them, will form a valuable part of that for you. I've often found Lent to be not just a time to give things up, but a time to adopt a new spiritual discipline; some have proved so beneficial that they now form part of my basic spiritual diet.

Yet I think there is still a necessary place for abstinence. Lent is also a time when we give something up. And as I have discovered the importance of my physicality and senses, I've become more aware of the part that giving up some aspect of our normal diet can play. When Jesus fasted in the wilderness for forty days and nights, it wasn't that he was just too busy to spare time and energy for food and drink. More importantly, neither was it some demonstration of his willpower or his supernatural strength. I'm aware that all too easily I can go into such a spiritual discipline to prove to myself or to God that I can do it. When I do that, the focus becomes me not God, and the exercise is worthless.

Jesus knew that abstaining from physical nourishment would bring him closer to God. And that's something I have found too. For a number of years, I followed a discipline of fasting from all food for an entire day each week during Lent. The day of the week varied, so as not to affront anyone hosting me by rejecting the food they offered. But there would always be at least one or two days when I could quietly avoid food without drawing attention to myself. I found that it was possible to divert my hunger for physical sustenance into a hunger for God. When my stomach rumbled or I felt the desire to eat, I took it as an invitation to pray. I was able to turn to the one who can satisfy my every need, not simply the demands of my belly. It served as a reminder that, apart from God, I can never truly have my needs satisfied, nor be nourished to grow into my full self. One year I offered to pray for anyone else who let me know they were fasting for Lent. And I asked them to remember me in their own prayers. A number of people did just that. I'm happy to make that same offer to any of you reading this. If you want me to pray for you on a day when you are fasting, and have a Twitter account, you can contact me at @bishmanchester.

What also surprised me was that fasting not only lifted up my eyes to God but also directed my gaze outwards to his creation. We don't have to do much more than switch on the TV or radio or open a newspaper to be confronted by the number of people going hungry in this world. They may be suffering from a failed harvest due to extreme weather or other effects of climate change, or they may be people in our own nation who haven't received the benefit payments they require in order to feed themselves and their children. Hunger surrounds us, and the discipline of fasting can help draw it to our attention. When I feel hungry myself, I just naturally become more aware of news items about hunger elsewhere. And then I can turn my prayers towards those whose stomachs are far emptier than my own, and reaffirm my commitment to supporting efforts to alleviate poverty and to reduce the negative impact of humanity on the world's climate. My prayer is both God-centred and centred on those most in need.

We tend to look at the story of Jesus fasting in the wilderness entirely through the lens of his battle with the devil. And yet when we read the story carefully, it is clear that his temptations come only towards the end of that period. For the vast majority of his time he is simply using his abstinence from food to assist him in preparing for his public ministry by building up the pattern of his own spiritual life. The devil visits him three times; God is with him far more than that. So I wish you well with your own Lenten discipline as we begin this season. May all that you take up and all that you give up draw you closer to the one in whose name you are doing it.

Gracious God,
your Son Jesus prayed for 40 days in the wilderness
as he sought your will for his way forward.
Be close to us when we face hard choices,
especially those which have a lasting impact on our life's journey.
Whisper your holy word into our ears,
that we might hear which way to go;
and forgive us when our deafness sets us on another path.
Grant this for the sake of him who suffered, died and rose for us:
Jesus Christ our Lord. Amen

Thursday

In his image

[The disciples of the Pharisees said to Jesus,] 'Tell us, then, what you think. Is it **lawful** to pay taxes to the emperor, or not?' But Jesus, **aware of** their malice, said, 'Why are you putting me to the test, you hypocrites? Show me the coin used for the tax.' And they brought him a denarius. Then he said to them, 'Whose head is this, and whose title?' They answered, 'The emperor's.' Then he said to them, 'Give therefore to the emperor the things that are the emperor's, and to God the things that are God's.'

MATTHEW 22:17–21

My art-and-craft skills have never been my strong point. At school I did well in most subjects, but my efforts at painting and drawing were pretty derisory. I was not immediately pleased when my class was told that our final year of sixth form was going to include compulsory metal- or woodwork. I opted for wood, probably because I thought I would do less damage that way. Three months later I was the proud possessor of a table, made out of old desktops, containing an inlaid wooden chessboard and supported on a single central leg. Over 40 years on, that table still has pride of place in our living room, and nobody has ever dared suggest it should be thrown out and replaced with something more elegant or well made. It's my own creation, fashioned by my own clumsy hands. It belongs to me in a way that nothing I have purchased will ever achieve. I'm not immune to either the errors in its construction or the damage wrought on it from living with me for four decades, but to my eyes it will always be a delight.

That table has taught me a lot about how I appear to God. I am his creation, fashioned by his own hand, just as my woodwork creation was fashioned by mine. His sense that I belong with him is no less than mine that the table belongs with me. There are some differences, but they are differences of degree not of kind.

For one, I like to think that the work involved in creating me has taken rather longer than a few school lessons' worth. I see God's work in creating each individual human being as stretching back to the very beginning of time. When God's word first exploded into matter and energy, time and space, some 14 billion years ago, that process of fashioning you and me was part of the purpose. As scripture says, even before we were in the womb God knew us. And while God's effort has produced billions of human beings on this one planet, and he alone knows what else, he would have gladly made the same effort even if you, or I, were the only result of his work. We can look at the stars in the sky, the intricacies of a flower or the beauty of a rainbow over a waterfall and know that God sees each and every one of us as worth it all.

Over the years I have done some limited work to keep my table in acceptable shape. I filled a crack that had opened through the wood's drying and shrinking a little in its early years. And I've sanded it down and revarnished it a couple of times, to remove some of the scratches and stains of family and vicarage life. But by and large the work was completed on the day my uncle came with me to school so that I could take it home in his van. By contrast, we are very much still works in progress. We need to let God continue to reshape and reform us. Not only does he repair our damage and gently smooth away some of our roughest edges, but from time to time more radical revision is needed. I'm old enough now to be able to look back over the trajectory of my life and catch a glimpse of his handiwork at different stages. He has enabled me to become who I am, and he is readying me for who I am yet to be.

When I turned up to the school workshops, ready if not entirely willing, the teacher gave me a handful of magazines to look through. Faced with page after page of designs, there was just something about the chess table that captured my imagination. It was far from the easiest project in the book – it required mastering a range of different skills – but the photograph of the finished product was compelling. What I produced did satisfactorily look like the image in the book, but it didn't, and was never intended to, resemble me. The glory of a human being lies not just in the fact that God has made us and that we belong with God, but also in the fact that we are fashioned in his image. When Jesus invites his questioners to look at the image on the coins used to pay Roman taxes, they see the head of Caesar. The coin bearing that design belonged to the Roman emperor. When he goes on immediately to tell them to 'give to God the things that are God's', I'm convinced that he has in mind our very selves. Because we are made in God's image, we are as much his as the coin is Caesar's.

God has been making us since the beginning of time; he fashions us still in each moment of our lives, seeking to form us ever more closely into his likeness. Wherever we may be, however far out of our comfort zone or away from home we are, we belong with him just as much as my table belongs to me, only more so. And while no doubt the table will be discarded and broken up after my death, our belonging with our creator will last into eternity.

> *Almighty God,*
> *We thank you that you rejoice in all of your creation,*
> *and have fashioned each one of us from the beginning.*
> *Help us this day and every day*
> *to recognise that we are made in your image*
> *and wonderfully crafted out of love.*
> *May we seek each day*
> *to grow ever more into your likeness,*
> *until we see you face-to-face. Amen*

Friday

A child of the Father

[Jesus said,] 'Is there anyone among you who, if your child asks for a fish, will give a snake instead of a fish? Or if the child asks for an egg, will give a scorpion? If you then, who are evil, know how to give good gifts to your children, how much more will the heavenly Father give the Holy Spirit to those who ask him!'

LUKE 11:11–13

I've learnt a lot about God by looking at other people. As part of that, I've sought to understand my relationship with God by reflecting on the relationships I have with those who are closest to me. I was fortunate enough to have a good dad, though sadly he died when I was in my early teens, and I can draw on my childhood experience to gain a better grasp of what it means to refer to God as my heavenly Father.

I also draw on my experience of the parent-child relationship from the other side. I have two children, both now grown up. I remember vividly the day our first child, our daughter, was born. After a somewhat dramatic morning – she was nearly born in the ambulance – I returned home just in time for the start of the church spring fair. I walked around the stalls in something of a daze, astounded at how different I felt simply because this new life had come into the world – a life for which I held a responsibility and that was, in at least a genetic sense, an extension of me beyond my physical body. It felt like a form of immortality. Whole sections of the Old Testament, where family and descent are so central, began to make sense to me in a way that they never had before. That bond has never lessened, even though both our children now live a couple of hundred miles away. We went through our full share of all the traumas and delights of family life, which drew us closer together. I am inordinately proud of their achievements and fiercely protective of their well-being.

I know that not everyone has had the fortune of receiving good parenting or been blessed with children to look after and care for. I'm sorry if what I'm writing here takes some of you back into difficult and hard places. But perhaps even the absence of love leaves a space that we can recognise for what ought, in a better world, to be there.

So when I seek to understand how God feels about me, I go back to my own experiences as both son and dad. I take all the best and finest of that, and I imagine it taken up to a greater order of magnitude. I belong with God with all the fierceness of my love for my own father and my children, only more so. I have had to forgive and to be forgiven, so I can begin to imagine what the one who is more forgiving than any human parent must be like. I have felt the bonds of love that have withstood the challenges and tribulations of family life and can begin to imagine a love far stronger even than that.

Jesus reminds us in Luke's gospel that if we, imperfect human beings, know not to give our child a snake when they ask for a fish or a scorpion when they ask for an egg, how much more will God give to us the things that are good for us, especially his Holy Spirit. I can relate that to my own experience of giving and receiving gifts, delighting at a child's handmade Christmas offering or the presents my father made for me with his own hands.

To know myself as a child of God, belonging with a Father whose image I bear and whose love and forgiveness are limitless, is the most amazing liberation. Like a young child learning a new skill, I can try things and fail; I can hurt myself and even others in the process. But the love that surrounds me and sustains me, the love that makes me bold enough to want to go on trying until I've got it right, remains undiminished. In my prayers I can picture and sense myself resting in the arms of the Father who loves me. I can feel the warmth of his smile, whether a pure smile of happiness at what I'm doing or a wry smile of forgiveness at my latest failing. I can hear the clear tones of his voice, assuring me that I am loved and doing so with an authority that leaves me with no possible doubt. Resting in my position as a child gives me the wherewithal to then go out and be the adult I need to be, for God's sake, in the world. Indeed, it gives me just enough to be able to face up to the specific nature of my calling as a bishop to be 'father in God' in my diocese.

Try, then, to spend a few minutes today reflecting on the best experiences of parenting you can bring to mind, and then let God be the parent and yourself the child. Let him speak to you the words you need most to hear from him, in the tones that leave his abiding love in no doubt. Then take that with you into whatever tasks lie before you and whichever relationships you are nurturing today.

Heavenly Father,
help us to trust you
as a child trusts a loving parent.
May we in turn prove worthy of trust,
that we may care diligently for all
who place their trust in us. Amen

Saturday

The one who defeats evil

War broke out in heaven; Michael and his angels fought against the dragon. The dragon and his angels fought back, but they were defeated, and there was no longer any place for them in heaven. The great dragon was thrown down, that ancient serpent, who is called the Devil and Satan, the deceiver of the whole world – he was thrown down to the earth, and his angels were thrown down with him.

REVELATION 12:7–9

It's not surprising that one of the earliest and most persistent Christian heresies has been the belief that God and the devil are almost equally balanced supernatural powers, fighting it out over the destiny of both individual human souls and the whole created order. Here on earth it can often feel that way. We can end up imagining ourselves as foot soldiers in this cosmic battle, ranged against both demonic powers and Satan's own earthly allies, fighting both for our own salvation and for the destiny of the universe.

Yet today's Bible passage and the weight of orthodox Christian faith offer us a very different account. We are not pawns in some metaphysical game of chess. The one to whom we belong has defeated evil. The temporal world may suffer under its death throes, but there is no uncertainty about the ultimate destiny before us. The challenge is to live not on the battlefield but rather in the assurance of victory won.

That might sound like a very abstract notion, but it's actually one of the most practical yardsticks I seek to live by. It's especially important for me to judge my words and deeds by it when I am most surrounded by the consequences of evil. One of the defining moments of my time as Bishop of Manchester came with the murder of 22 people in a suicide bomb attack. The perpetrator saw himself as a soldier in a war against British society. While his immediate aim was to kill and maim as many as possible, his long-term objective was to sow seeds of distrust among the people of one of Europe's most diverse modern cities. He would have hoped, perhaps even prayed, to provoke acts of retaliation to divide our different faith groups. He wanted to drag us into hatred. I cannot comprehend what his first encounter with God, after he detonated his device, must have been like.

As bishop, I was called to speak up for Manchester on the day after the attack. I was able to say to the crowds gathered in the city centre, and to many millions watching or listening around the world, that light is stronger than darkness and love is stronger than hate. Love wins, and engaging in expressions of love across our community, rather than seeking scapegoats for revenge, is the true means to show our defiance. I had to say the words, but they would have come across as empty and hollow unless I truly believed them. What I felt, as I opened my mouth, was the presence of the Holy Spirit within me. That presence gave me the final bit of reassurance I needed to be able to speak with complete confidence. I belong with a God who has conquered. I believe that the victory of love was completed 2,000 years ago on a cross outside Jerusalem. And I can speak out of that belief.

In some ways, the big and blatant evil of a terror attack has a more obvious response than the small and banal evils that pervade our daily lives. Indeed, human beings are often very good at responding well to a tragedy but far less proficient at maintaining our ground under constant low-level attack. We are like the stone that stands firm under the impact of a hammer but can be eroded away to nothing by a steady drip of water over many millennia. Community harmony faces a more insidious attack from a constant trickle of petty racist incidents, anti-Semitic and Islamophobic media comments, and the abuse of people on the grounds of gender, disability and sexuality. Bullying, in the workplace, at school and at home, along with gangs, drugs and modern slavery, may damage us far more than the isolated extremist can. The need for us to speak, act and believe in the victory of love is both harder and more vital here.

The stained-glass windows of the chapel of King's College, Cambridge, where I studied mathematics for five years and grew in my faith, are one of the finest examples of art in glass in the world. During World War II the historic panes were removed and taken to a place of safety, lest they become victims of a bomb blast. One day, the dean of the chapel drew my attention to a feature in one particular window. It depicted the devil, who, apart from a tiny detail of horns and hooves, looked every bit like a genial fellow of the college, someone you might expect to sit next to at supper and share a glass of wine with. I learnt then that we need to be most on our guard against evil not when it dresses itself up in a suicide vest or military uniform but when it poses as one of us. Then, it is only the firmness of our belonging with Christ that will enable us to see the imposter for who they are.

> *Lord Jesus Christ,*
> *by your cross, you have defeated the powers of darkness.*
> *Help us to live in the assurance of that victory*
> *and to resist those remnants of evil*
> *that continue to distort your creation. Amen*

Sunday

The challenge of choices

Then Jesus was led up by the Spirit into the wilderness to be tempted by the devil. He fasted for forty days and forty nights, and afterwards he was famished. The tempter came and said to him, 'If you are the Son of God, command these stones to become loaves of bread.' But he answered, 'It is written, "One does not live by bread alone, but by every word that comes from the mouth of God."'

MATTHEW 4:1–4

I wanted to study for ordination somewhere that was unlike anywhere I'd lived before. I chose Birmingham, and I found myself thrown into the life of a big, cosmopolitan city. It was fascinating to live alongside people with backgrounds very different from my own, not least those from other religious and ethnic groups. I got myself attached to an inner-city parish and loved it dearly. It was there that I first came across some of the depths of poverty that exist within our society. The church did brilliant work among isolated older people, marginalised teenagers and others in need. As well as the clergy, there were other workers, paid and volunteer, who made all this amazing stuff happen. It opened my eyes to how vital the work that churches do is in meeting human need, especially for those who have fallen through the holes in the safety net that society ought to provide. We even had a small sheltered housing scheme, a partnership with a local housing association, which provided homes and support through 15 flats, which were next door to the church building. I went back one evening to my college wondering whether I would be more use to God working directly with the neediest than by pursuing ordination. Had I got my calling wrong?

Jesus is at his most human in stories like that of his 40 days in the wilderness. He too is tempted, just as we are. The thing that always strikes me about these temptations is that none of them are to do anything evil or bad in themselves.

Jumping off the temple roof and surviving would give the most tremendous boost to his ministry. He could preach and teach, secure that his credentials as being sent by God had been proven in a spectacular fashion.

Or he could take the role of what we would now call political leadership. He could have been the wisest and most honourable leader of any nation ever: stopping wars; eradicating injustice; rewarding goodness.

Or he could turn stones to bread. I never see this as simply about satisfying his own intense hunger. He could have made bread enough for everyone, way beyond what he accomplishes with the feeding of the 5,000. He had the power to eradicate hunger, and with it poverty, once and for all. And yet this, along with the other two offers placed before him, clearly comes couched as temptation.

My brief for my final year of training was to spend most of it in the parish, but to reflect on my experiences from time to time, through pieces of work I would share with my tutor. So I wrote an essay. I've entirely forgotten the details of the content of it, but the title was 'Why I am not a social worker'. It wasn't disparaging in any way to members of that profession. Indeed, by then I had seen enough of them at work to realise how vital their role, and the work of others, was in enabling people to survive and thrive in the face of the grinding pressures of inner-city poverty. Rather, it was about my recognising that the specific calling God had given to me could not be fulfilled in such a career. Right at the heart of who I was being shaped into, through both my deepening spiritual life and my theological training, was the role of priest. I would feed the broken and needy, but the bread I would offer would be the broken body of Christ.

Making that choice has not prevented me from being actively involved in caring for those in need down the years since. Nor has it been the one and only time when I have had to wrestle with the temptation to go down some path that is good in itself, just not the one for me to travel. Indeed, I feel that I belong with Jesus in the wilderness, seeking the direction that comes from God. What happens for Jesus is that, as he contemplates each of Satan's offers, a phrase from scripture comes to the forefront of his mind. These aren't the only biblical words with potential relevance to the situation. Each time, the devil has offered a quote that could be construed as being in favour of yielding to his approaches. What matters is that the phrase which underpins Jesus' resistance comes not from the tempter but from the depth of his own prayer and fasting. Placed there by God himself, Jesus' spiritual discipline allows it to emerge to the surface of his mind and then be seen as the authentic response that it is.

When we face hard challenges of choice, Jesus faces them with us, and we belong with him. He knows what we are going through because he himself has been there, in the wilderness. He offers us three vital clues as to how to face decisions – we pray, we fast and we listen for the voice of God bringing some word of scripture to us with an inner authority. Sometimes it may take a full 40 days or even longer. Unlike Jesus, we won't get every choice right, but we can be assured that he who faced the wilderness continues to forgive and love us, we who belong with him.

Lord Jesus Christ,
in the wilderness you rejected false choices
and followed with firmness the will of the Father.
Be with us when we are faced with complex alternatives
or have difficult life decisions to make.
So guide us,
that we may find a path
along which you will be glad to accompany us. Amen

Monday

Jesus the teacher

The next day John again was standing with two of his disciples, and as he watched Jesus walk by, he exclaimed, 'Look, here is the Lamb of God!' The two disciples heard him say this, and they followed Jesus. When Jesus turned and saw them following, he said to them, 'What are you looking for?' They said to him, 'Rabbi' (which translated means Teacher), 'where are you staying?' He said to them, 'Come and see.' They came and saw where he was staying, and they remained with him that day.

JOHN 1:35–39

I can still picture the faces of many of those who have taught me. Each in their way has influenced not only what I know but also what I value and how I behave. A sixth-form maths teacher instilled in me a desire not just to find the right answer but to get there by the most elegant and simple route. A university lecturer kindled in me a love for the most abstract of concepts. A college tutor helped me to develop confidence as a public speaker. What's more, that practice of having a teacher who guides and inspires me didn't end when I knelt before a bishop to be ordained; it continued through the more experienced clergy with whom I worked in my early adult years, through to the diocesan bishop who was my first colleague after my own episcopal consecration and on to the professor who leads the group of scholars with which I do much of my theological research and reflection. To have a teacher is not to lack confidence in my own capabilities and experience, but it is to realise that I am still learning.

The title of teacher, or rabbi, is applied to Jesus a lot in the gospels. As with my own experience, it means much more than someone who imparts information. In fact, there is little suggestion that Jesus followed the widespread tradition of teaching his disciples large chunks of material that they then had to recite back to him accurately. We only have one prayer that he appears to have taught them to use. And even the Lord's Prayer itself reads more like an example or an outline around which anyone can build their own particular petitions.

Rather, the disciples accompanied Jesus from place to place as he ministered and were increasingly invited and entrusted to prepare the ground in the towns and villages he intended to visit. With greater or lesser degrees of success, during his earthly ministry and afterwards, they copied the kinds of things they had seen him doing. They took on the values that he espoused and demonstrated the love and forgiveness that lay at the heart of his teaching. Through this they became the community that convinced large chunks of humanity to become his followers too.

At the heart of this lay the fact that Jesus had never actually stopped being their teacher. Before his crucifixion, he had assured them, as recorded in John's gospel, that he would dwell within them. Matthew tells us that Jesus' final meeting with his disciples after his resurrection contained a promise to be with them until the end of the age. Jesus was true to his word. He went on being their teacher, and Christians around the world find him exercising that same role in their lives today.

A few years ago there was a fashion, especially among teenage Christians, for wearing a plastic wristband with the letters WWJD on it. The initials stood for 'What would Jesus do?' and were a simple invitation for the wearer to imagine how Christ would respond to their situation before they fixed on a course of action. The fashion was treated by some with disdain. It was alleged to be simplistic, not least by seeking to find a direct answer from Jesus to a situation that could never have occurred during his earthly ministry. Nevertheless, I believe a great truth lies at its heart. If Jesus is our teacher, and we belong with him in a relationship as his first disciples did, then like them we should seek to copy his behaviour, even if that requires an effort of imaginative prayer rather than direct observation.

Moreover, that attempt to imagine the action and reaction of Jesus in a particular situation takes place in a much wider context. The Christian who takes Christ as teacher is seeking to follow the pattern of his teaching and the example of his life, not just in response to some isolated ethical dilemma but day in and day out. Through the imitation of Christ, a discipline that goes back down the centuries, we are slowly but surely transformed into his image, just as in the ancient world the goal of many a pupil was to become ever more like their master. As we grow in the likeness of Jesus, the work of behaving as he would becomes ever more natural to us, sustained by repetition as well as by our abiding relationship with him in each present moment.

Come, Lord Jesus,
and be our teacher,
as you taught the people of Israel long ago.
May we so follow your good example
that we grow ever more in your likeness,
until we take our place in heaven. Amen

Tuesday

The one who makes his home within us

Jesus said to them, 'Very truly, I tell you, unless you eat the flesh of the Son of Man and drink his blood, you have no life in you. Those who eat my flesh and drink my blood have eternal life, and I will raise them up on the last day; for my flesh is true food and my blood is true drink. Those who eat my flesh and drink my blood abide in me, and I in them.'
JOHN 6:53–56

I grew up with a conventional notion of God as 'out there', separate from and quite other than me. He was a God who watched over my doings and would determine on their basis to reward or punish me when the final account was totted up. He wasn't a very believable God, and I rejected my image of him somewhere in my early teens. The faith I came back to a few years later was very different: here was a God not of observation but relationship. And I was blown over by John's description that, in some sense, this God whom I had rediscovered and the Jesus whom I met in the pages of scripture and in my prayers had not only a home in heaven but also a dwelling place inside of me.

This was a revelation that impacted directly on my understanding of the Eucharist. Every time I ate and drank of the sacrament, some small portion of the molecules within the bread and wine became part of my own body and blood. I had to live my life as one within whom Christ himself dwelt, a reality of which the residue of the sacrament within me was a sign and symbol.

Alongside this, I began to develop a stronger sense of what I could only believe was the Holy Spirit at work deep within me. It was the Spirit who gave me the strength to do things beyond my own capability, and the same Spirit who helped me to be a little more likely to choose the right thing from among the options available.

Part of the challenge is that whatever I believe about myself in this respect, I must equally believe to be true with regard to my fellow Christians. They too are hosts of Christ and temples of the Holy Spirit. If I give reverence to the God who dwells within me, I must give equal reverence to the God who dwells in you. Some years ago, an Anglican nun who was leading a retreat on which I was a participant encouraged us to greet our fellow retreatants with the Indian 'namaste'. She explained that in religious circles this is seen as the part of God within me paying reverence to the part of God within you. I rather liked the idea. Once I acknowledge that my God is in you, I have to treat you with a degree of respect and reverence that may not otherwise appeal to me. Because we both belong with him through his indwelling, we cannot avoid a deeper belonging to one another, even when that is hard going.

One of my colleagues has a very helpful way of supporting this. She goes to the enigmatic story of Jacob wrestling with the angel. When his assailant demands to be released, Israel, as he will become known, replies, 'I will not let you go, unless you bless me' (Genesis 32:26). To recognise the divine within those who appear as our adversaries is one of the hardest challenges that faces Christians. At its heart lies a determination to remain engaged with those who share our faith but with whom we disagree most profoundly. The image of two wrestlers is particularly apposite, because it suggests we should not merely yield to the other's view nor agree to differ and then ignore the conflict between our views.

It's an image that acts against the temptation to write others off over some doctrinal or ethical difference. Sadly, the succumbing to that temptation has been a decisive factor in the fragmentation of the

Christian church over the centuries since the Reformation. Once we have ceased to recognise the presence of God in one another, we are all too ready to see our opponents as agents of the devil. Some of the polemical works of art produced by both Catholic and Protestant sides during the 16th and 17th centuries show this graphically.

Most recently, I've become more aware that the God who dwells within me in this life is playing a vital part in preparing me for life beyond. That intermingling of our two selves here on earth acts as a foretaste of the intimacy of relationship and indwelling that will be eternity and heaven. I can sense the flow of divine energy that comes from within me, reaching out beyond and returning, like electricity moving through a circuit. For now, it flows through my body, and at my deepest moments of prayer I can feel the force of it. At some point in the future my physical body will no longer need to be part of the circulation, but my self will remain totally connected. The God who has made his home and belonging within me will have come and brought me to make my eternal home within him.

Lord Jesus Christ,
may my heart be ever open
to welcome you in.
Dwell within me this day and always,
and grant me the gift
to recognise your presence in others,
especially in those from whom I differ most. Amen

Wednesday

Jesus who heals us

Now Simon's mother-in-law was in bed with a fever, and they told [Jesus] about her at once. He came and took her by the hand and lifted her up. Then the fever left her, and she began to serve them. That evening, at sunset, they brought to him all who were sick or possessed with demons. And the whole city was gathered around the door. And he cured many who were sick with various diseases.

MARK 1:30–34

In every place and generation there is a tendency for us to understand the actions of Jesus in line with the prevailing tenets of our culture. So when we come to the healing miracles of the gospel, it is not surprising that they are subjected to that sort of interpretation. When Jesus enables the dumb to speak, the deaf to hear or the lame to walk, sermons often focus on the language and theology of wholeness. Christ takes those who are damaged in some way and enables them to become more fully the complete human beings they were intended to be. It's an important insight. It grasps the clear message that all life on earth is limited and broken and that God wills us to a destiny in which all such limitation is removed. We can become fully in his image as he intended.

Indeed, we live in a society where we are all encouraged, perhaps even commanded, to reach our full potential. All manner of therapies and treatments are theoretically available (provided we can access or pay for them). The advertising industry suggests to us that a combination of the right products and services will enable us to reach something close to earthly perfection. TV programmes bring before us the lives of the richest, most beautiful and most successful.

The implication is that if we only applied ourselves, tried hard enough and seized our chances, we too could have what they've got.

Who defines perfection ? ?

Yet, putting it into words helps me to realise how hopeless such a hope really is. The search for perfection lies at an impossible reach from the lives of most of the people on this planet, and it always has. Poverty, prejudice, war and corruption continue to exact their toll, especially on those who live in developing countries. These same people have little access to the basic health services many of us take for granted. The fight to improve the lot of the world's marginalised is both theirs and ours, and it remains urgent. But the goal of achieving wholeness in this life remains a false one.

The attraction of the wholeness approach to the healing miracles may be that it is a sufficiently vague concept to bypass the problem of why only some are made well. Yet that remains the scandal and the challenge of the gospel accounts. Not everybody is healed all the time. Three years of Jesus' earthly ministry did not eradicate blindness, paralysis or any other common condition from Israel. Is God simply unjust and unfair, bestowing favours on a chosen few while the many continue to suffer?

I find that I need to start somewhere else, with my understanding of belonging in Christ. Because I am his, and his will for me is perfect, I believe that he is working within me to bring a fulfilment that includes my wholeness. Yet I don't expect to see that in this earthly life. Indeed, I've reached an age where I can only anticipate my bodily health undergoing deterioration as the years pass. My mental faculties, too, lie at risk. I've visited too many people over the years who have spent their final years with dementia, failing to recognise their nearest and dearest, sometimes hardly recognisable themselves as their former personalities. To be healed is not to be spared all this, but to know that it cannot destroy me. The one to whom I belong will bring me through it. The sign and proof of that lies in the healing miracles of the Bible, just as the proof of God's preservation of his creation lies in the rainbow.

The kingdom of God resides within Jesus, and wherever he travels through the holy land we read stories of that kingdom overflowing into the world around him. The blind see; the deaf hear; the dead are raised. It is not that these specific individuals are of greater merit than the many others who might equally have benefitted; it is that they are the ones touched by the presence of the kingdom of God in Jesus. In him the reality of eternity erupts into this world, bringing healing in its wake. And it does so because it is not just individuals like you and me who belong with Christ, but the whole of creation. Life in all its fullness is within him; even if he wanted to, he could not contain it all.

Religious art sometimes depicts this by the way it shows the background in pictures of Jesus. The ground under his feet is often greener than elsewhere. Flowers bloom and trees burst into leaf around him in a very visible contrast to what surrounds other characters in the same artwork. Pictures of Jesus after his resurrection particularly abound in such artistic depiction, pressing the point that the Easter Christ is especially full of this new and perfected life. To him the whole created order belongs. The more deeply I dwell with him now, the more I can anticipate that final reality, notwithstanding my many physical and other imperfections.

Heavenly Father,
thank you for your power to heal.
Grant that we may know the gift of your healing,
both in this life and into eternity,
so that we place not our trust in human claims,
but turn always and only to you,
to bring us to perfection
in Jesus Christ. Amen

Thursday

Forgiveness

The Pharisees, who were lovers of money, heard all [Jesus said], and they ridiculed him. So he said to them, 'You are those who justify yourselves in the sight of others; but God knows your hearts; for what is prized by human beings is an abomination in the sight of God.'

LUKE 16:14–15

I was in the middle of a theological argument with my curate. We came from very different churchmanship traditions, and such conversations were not at all uncommon. I forget what it was I had just said, but his answer has remained with me ever since: 'Just because you're cleverer than me and can argue better doesn't mean you're always right and I'm always wrong.' It was both an accurate and astute observation. I have always been able to think quickly, to assemble and deploy an argument and to find the best riposte. It gives the impression of my being in the right somewhat more often than is the case.

Not least, that aspect of my personality has at times made it harder for me to grasp my need for forgiveness. Like the Pharisees in today's Bible reading, I grew up being able to justify whatever I had done in the face of criticism. Whatever act I had committed or deed I had failed to do, I would always have a plausible explanation, one that obviated any need for apology or admission of wrongdoing on my part. It really wasn't good for me. At an intellectual level I accepted that I, along with every other human being, was a sinner who needed God's forgiveness. I prayed the Lord's Prayer often enough to be reminded that asking for and granting forgiveness is the hallmark of how human beings need to behave towards each other. It was just that on any particular occasion, like the Pharisees of old, I could convince myself, even if not those around me, that my actions had been beyond reproach. I was by all accounts a capable and gifted parish priest, but there was a whole chunk of what life in Christ is about that I was continuing to avoid.

The breakthrough came when I spent the best part of a year having weekly meetings with a therapist. Over the months it became a safe place where I was able to let down my guard and explore the reality of who I was and the forces that had formed me in a particular way. Somewhere in that I discovered that saying I was sorry made me feel better than going on justifying my position. And it made the person I had offended against feel better too. Rather than being an admission of weakness, penitence freed me up and allowed me to move on. I was stronger and better for it. Constant self-justification wore down my belonging with others; apologising and asking for forgiveness built it up again.

While thanks must go to my therapist, it is Christ himself to whom I give the greater credit. I discovered that, in him, the things for which I was saying I was sorry were already forgiven; some indeed had been forgiven long before. Crucially, I found that forgiveness can come before repentance. Sometimes that's the way it absolutely has to be. Even with other human beings, the knowledge that I am already forgiven is what gives me the courage to admit my fault. Without that, I can fall victim to the concern that any admission on my part will be amplified and exaggerated in order to do me harm that far outweighs my sin. My own experience of forgiveness also has to be what I offer to others. I need to find ways of assuring those who have offended me that we still belong to one another in Christ. I need to forgive them in my heart, and perhaps in my words, before they ask, in order that they might be able to apologise.

I'm sure that the need for forgiveness to come before repentance lies at the heart of why politicians and others in public life find it so difficult to admit even the smallest mistake. Their fear that an apology will be weaponised against them is entirely well founded. Whole careers have been lost as the consequence of a single mistake. We see it, too, in areas of our common life that have become increasingly litigious in recent years. One of the impediments to improvement in our health service is that any practitioner who admits a mistake risks being on the receiving end of a hefty legal claim. And yet it is much harder to learn from mistakes if we are not allowed to admit them. The defensive and protective attitude in most of our major institutions when it comes to matters of past safeguarding failures comes from a similar concern.

To know that I belong with a God who has already forgiven me is what allows me to let my guard down and permit myself to see how far short I have fallen. Only then can I truly and fully repent, acknowledging my failings both to him and to those I have let down. I need to know that I will not belong any less to him in consequence of my errors, even the most culpable of them.

This isn't something I can attain purely by intellectual assent; it needs to be experienced over and over again until it becomes an ever-stronger dimension to my core being in Christ. That experience is not primarily achieved through a forensic analysis of where I have gone wrong. God already knows my sins, and I can bear only a certain quantity of knowledge about them. Rather, the fact and assurance of forgiveness are found in simply being with Christ. It is silent meditation in his presence, sitting with him in quiet and absorbing the love that emanates from him that settles my fretful spirit. Then, and only then, do I know that I am truly forgiven.

Almighty God,
you stand willing to absolve our misdoings
long before we can find the courage to repent.
Help us to abide in the assurance of forgiveness,
that we may never seek to justify our sins
but be ready to confess our failings
and so dwell more deeply in your love. Amen

Friday

The God who feeds us

**One of his disciples, Andrew, Simon Peter's brother, said to
[Jesus], 'There is a boy here who has five barley loaves and
two fish. But what are they among so many people?' Jesus
said, 'Make the people sit down.' Now there was a great deal
of grass in the place; so they sat down, about five thousand
in all. Then Jesus took the loaves, and when he had given
thanks, he distributed them to those who were seated; so
also the fish, as much as they wanted.**

JOHN 6:8–11

Some years ago a colleague invited me out for a meal. The venue was
quite prestigious, and I felt at least a little flattered by it. The food
and drink were good and the conversation pleasant and warm. Then
he came to the crux of the matter. There was something he wanted
to ask me to do. It was a plausible suggestion, as it fitted in well with
some of my interests and built on my experience. But it would have
required quite a significant change to the current focus of my time
and energies. I try to be open to any such approaches, seeking to
discern whether the invitation is actually coming not just from the
person with me but from God. Some of the most fundamental shifts
in my life and ministry have come about in such ways. Yet this I knew,
almost from the moment he raised the subject, was not something
that felt right for me.

The problem I faced was how to put that message across. It would
have been much easier to dismiss a letter or email or even a phone
conversation. But here we were, dining together, him as the host
and me as the guest. That created a particular connection between
us, one which made rejecting his suggestion far harder. I did say

'No', but it was far from easy. I had to take his proposal with all the seriousness that the bond formed over our meal demanded.

The account of Jesus feeding an enormous crowd of people is the only miracle story that features in all four gospels. It clearly meant a great deal to the early Christian church, across a wide variety of places and contexts. It can't just have been the scale of the miracle; after all, Jesus did plenty of more remarkable things than this. I guess it has something to do with the importance of food and the bonds it builds between us.

I'm convinced the story is far more than Jesus simply having compassion on a hungry crowd. Yes, they had been listening in rapt attention to his words for some hours, and they were indeed some distance away from being able to purchase food. But this was not a society where three full meals a day could be counted on. Many of his listeners would have been quite accustomed to having to skip physical sustenance from time to time. And all would have been familiar with the fasting days and practices of the Jewish faith. They could have eaten when they got home and been little the worse for it. There has to be a deeper reason.

What lies at the heart of this story is that the five thousand are eating both with Jesus and with one another, and that this shared meal forms a bond between them. Their relationships are both different and closer afterwards. They have not just been present at a unique and amazing event; they have accepted food there, too. It isn't coincidence that some of the most elaborate eating and drinking traditions and ceremonies across many cultures are associated with weddings. Indeed, some of the Asian wedding ceremonies I have attended involved a whole series of formal meals over several days, with many of the same people present. In marriage a new belonging is being formed and celebrated, not just between two individuals but between their respective families and their friends. These are the people whose support and encouragement they will need over the years to come. Those who were present and shared the loaves and fishes will return to their communities knowing that they share something special and abiding with everyone who partook of the meal with them. They belong together in a new and deeper way.

And they belong with Jesus, too. He takes the role of the host, giving the bread and fish to the disciples to distribute. By accepting his hospitality, they are allowing themselves to be formed into a new relationship with him, too. The words he has earlier spoken, which they would have already been mentally digesting, are given added force by the food he offers. When they return to their towns, villages and farms and are confronted by the demands and pressures of everyday life, they will remember and give greater weight to his teaching because they have received the loaves and fishes.

And yet there is one twist in the tale. John places this story close to where he is developing his Eucharistic theology, with Jesus speaking of how his followers will eat of his body. We can see the miracle as a precursor of the Eucharist, which strengthens our belonging with one another and with Christ. Yet when we do so, we need to remember the little boy who provides the food Jesus takes and multiplies. In my own church tradition, the bread and wine are brought up to the altar by representatives of the congregation. They are sometimes referred to as 'the gifts of the people', and we speak of how they are the 'work of human hands' as well as the bounty of creation. While Jesus is the host and master of the feast, you and I are not simply passive recipients. We are invited to bring our own offering, which may then be multiplied into something far beyond our expectations or imagination. We are part of how this deeper and greater belonging with one another and with Christ is made real.

Lord Jesus Christ,
as you fed the crowds in Galilee long ago,
so feed us today,
and grant that we may in turn
be the means by which others are fed. Amen

Saturday

The God of eternity

Then I saw a new heaven and a new earth; for the first heaven and the first earth had passed away, and the sea was no more. And I saw the holy city, the new Jerusalem, coming down out of heaven from God, prepared as a bride adorned for her husband. And I heard a loud voice from the throne saying, 'See, the home of God is among mortals. He will dwell with them; they will be his peoples, and God himself will be with them.'

REVELATION 21:1–3

I'd been reading a piece of academic theology that was making a case for why Christians should let go of any expectation of an afterlife and recognise that the promises Jesus Christ brings to his disciples are of a life lived to its full here on earth – that this, here and now, is the only eternity we get. I put down the book and switched on the TV to see stories of famine in Africa, wars in the Middle East and the prevalence of deaths from treatable diseases across the developing world. The discrepancy between what I was seeing and what I had just read hit me hard. I could imagine how such a theology might make sense from the perspective of a comfortable seat in the well-appointed study of a tenured academic. I could not see how it could even begin to make sense to that great majority of the world's population, in this and in every other generation, for whom life is short, painful and deeply unfair.

That, after all, was why the Israelites in the centuries before Jesus gradually realised that life must have something more substantial than the shady notion of Sheol beyond it. Where was the justice for those who had lived lives of piety and faithfulness to God, only to be killed at a young age defending Israel from its oppressors? Surely there must be a day of judgement and a moment when those whose lives had been cut short would rise again.

Images of eternity are notoriously hard to capture and describe within a finite space. Most of the descriptions of heaven I have heard or read come across as at best banal. Some sound so profoundly boring that to dwell there forever would feel more like hell.

And yet I believe. I believe both because of the call of justice and because I cannot imagine that the God who has made me, who loves and forgives me, wants anything less than to bring me into his eternal presence. I belong with him, and everything I experience of him tells me that you and I are far too precious in his sight for him to simply consign us to vanish forever.

So when I try to imagine my destiny beyond this present life, I look not to clouds and harps, or even the imagery of the book of Revelation, but to the one who is my God and my all. Heaven is not some place within which God dwells, for that would be to make it greater than him. Rather, heaven exists within God himself, and, as I journey through life exploring my relationship with him, I will discover more about the nature of heaven along the way. In this life he greets me and knows me as a unique individual, one who belongs with him and who is capable of responding to his love for me with my own love of him. The closeness that will bind us in heaven will, I'm sure, far surpass any closeness possible on earth, but the essential nature of my selfhood will not simply be absorbed and dissipated; rather, it will be held and retained within that greater unity. I will still be me, though I will be the fullness of me never completely achieved before.

It's a basic principle of mathematics, the subject I first graduated in, that if two objects are both close to a third, they must also be close to each other. In some ways the scariest aspect of heaven is not that I shall be close to the Christ who already knows me fully and more intimately than any human being. The hard part is that I shall also be close to and known by those whom I have sinned against in this life. We shall belong together in a place without secrets. My poor motives, my selfishness, my shortcomings in love will be known not only by God but also by the wider population of heaven. And I will know theirs. How will I not want to flee to the darkest corner, to hide myself from my shame?

Yet just as our shared belonging with God will bring us into that challenging proximity, so it will provide the means to abide within it. I will see those who in this life I have seen only dimly, not as I see them now but as God sees them. And they will see me, not merely with their human eyes but through the eyes of Christ. His love and his forgiveness will become ours. Scars will be healed, enmities will dissolve in unity and tears will be wiped away.

Eternal God,
you call us to follow you,
both in this life and beyond.
Grant that we may ever travel secure in the faith
that your love is stronger than the grave,
and that we shall live with you forever. Amen

Week 2

BELONGING IN RELATIONSHIPS

Many years before I began to develop the model of belonging that underpins this book, I became convinced that, as you and I are made in God's own image, the relationships we have with other people throw light on our relationship with the one we worship. In particular, the relationships we have with those who mean the most to us, our families and friends, should be icons of what it means to be in relationship with God.

Here, as elsewhere, I draw on my personal experience. What do I learn about God from being a husband, a grandfather and a brother? How do relationships at work and in the wider community help us to belong as Christians? And what does it mean to remain in relationship with those whose earthly journey is done?

Sunday

Nicodemus

Jesus answered him, 'Very truly, I tell you, no one can see the kingdom of God without being born from above.' Nicodemus said to him, 'How can anyone be born after having grown old? Can one enter a second time into the mother's womb and be born?' Jesus answered, 'Very truly, I tell you, no one can enter the kingdom of God without being born of water and Spirit.'

JOHN 3:3–5

Over the past week and a half we have been reflecting on what it means to belong with God and Jesus. During this second week in Lent our focus moves on to how we belong in our human relationships and local communities. The story of Jesus' encounter with Nicodemus, which is read in many churches on this Sunday, brings our dual belonging into clear focus, and so provides something of a bridge between our themes.

Nicodemus is an important and influential citizen, a man deeply embedded in the ruling structures of Jewish society as well as in the religious traditions and practices of his people. He knows the importance of ancestry in Judaism; he is a descendent of Abraham and thus an inheritor of the promises made by God to his forefather. John's gospel repeatedly challenges the Jewish appeal to physical descent, and this exchange between Jesus and his night-time visitor allows the evangelist to develop this theme. Nicodemus cannot rely solely on his genealogy; he needs a second birth 'from above'. It is only as a child of God, born of the Spirit as well as of the flesh, that he will be able to take his place in God's kingdom.

The notion of being 'born again' is one that plays a central role in many parts of the Christian spectrum. For some it succinctly describes a moment of conversion, when a sudden and radical change of life comes about from accepting Jesus Christ as Lord. The change is so abrupt that it compares with starting life all over again, as though everything up to that point were dead and gone. For others it is a more gradual process, the slow realisation of something that has been there all along, perhaps from earliest childhood, but not articulated or named. My own story falls somewhere between those two poles, as over a period of weeks and months, in my late teens, I became more aware of the truth of the gospels and the reality of Jesus in my life.

One of my greatest fears, as that process of change took place within me, was whether it would drive a wedge between me and the human relationships, with family and friends, which were important to me. By contrast, what I found was that my human belonging and my new-found belonging with God were able to develop hand in hand. Having God in my life made me a better friend and family member. I resisted the immediate temptation to drift into an all-consuming Christian subculture, and I've avoided it ever since. I rejoice in the rich variety of relationships I have with friends and colleagues of all faiths and none.

I also discovered that Christians are not called, by their belonging with God, to set themselves apart from wider society, but to live fully within it, as a force for good. The more deeply I belong with God, the more deeply I belong with that part of his creation that surrounds me.

At the end of Jesus' response to his visitor, John moves the story on without telling us how Nicodemus responded. It's only several chapters later that we find out that Jesus' words have hit home. Towards the end of John 7, the argument is being made by some in the crowd that Jesus cannot be the Messiah because he doesn't have the right ancestry. He's a Galilean, not a clear descendent of King David. It's Nicodemus who steps in to calm things down when there are suggestions that Jesus should be arrested, and he even has his own heritage challenged in response. It's noteworthy that neither Nicodemus nor John chooses to defend Jesus by producing the family trees linking him to David, which both Matthew and Luke provide. That would be a distraction; it would risk placing emphasis back on to physical descent when what matters above all is our spiritual parentage.

Yet Nicodemus is not called by Jesus to choose between following him and continuing to play an important role in the life of Jerusalem and the nation. He can be both the child of his mother's womb and also of the Spirit. We encounter him one final time in John's gospel. After the crucifixion is over, we read that Nicodemus arrives at the tomb provided by Joseph of Arimathea. He brings a large quantity of spices, about a hundred pounds, with which the two men prepare Jesus' body in line with Jewish custom (John 19:38–42). It's a short but moving passage, at the end of that momentous day, in which Nicodemus shows himself to be both a descendent of Abraham and a child of God. His human belonging and his spiritual belonging each have their part to play in how he will follow the man he first met in secret one dark night.

Lord Jesus Christ,
you revealed to Nicodemus
that he must be born from above.
Grant that we, too,
may be children of both earthly and heavenly parentage,
serving you and humanity,
to the glory of the Father. Amen

Monday

Being a grandparent

I am reminded of your sincere faith, a faith that lived first in your grandmother Lois and your mother Eunice and now, I am sure, lives in you.
2 TIMOTHY 1:5

Outside of genealogical lists, grandparents don't play a huge role in the Bible. Given the much lower levels of life expectancy 2,000 years ago and beyond, that's hardly surprising, even though people married and bore children at a somewhat earlier age than nowadays. So when I became a grandfather for the first time, in 2016, I had nothing like the same amount of scriptural material to reflect on as had been the case 29 years earlier when our daughter was born. Becoming a grandad has also been a slower process of change than was parenthood. There isn't that huge, life-changing set of responsibilities, 24 hours a day, to be taken on board. And, as our daughter and her family live several hours away from us, I'm involved less often. So it has only been since around my grandson's second birthday, when he began to refer to me as 'Grandad', that I have started to discover what it means to belong with somebody in that way.

The surprising thing is that it has made me think about the way I belong with God in a new light, too. I've learned that an important way in which a relationship is sustained is through periods of intense closeness that punctuate the times when we are apart. Leo and I don't need to see each other every day in order to care for each other, love each other and enjoy one another's company. We fall naturally back into our relationship each time we meet, even if that has been some weeks or months ago – a gap over which he will have continued to grow and develop. We pick up our games and activities and know how to be around each other. When he gets older, I expect we will talk from time to time on the telephone, but for now we stick to relating face-to-face.

I find parallels between these periods together and the times when I go away on retreat. Spending time intensely focused on being in the presence of God has a vital role to play in sustaining my relationship with him during the rest of my life. Later in this book, I explore elsewhere how for many people, relating to God is most readily achieved through a similar focus on big, special events, such as festivals, regionally themed holidays and pilgrimages.

Part of the joy of grandparenthood is the many things that I'm not responsible for. It's more than simply being able to hand the little one back to be somebody else's responsibility. The fact that it's not down to me to get him dressed in the morning, sort out his food and drink, bath him and persuade him to go to bed, except if his parents ask me to on a specific occasion, means that the agenda for our time together is very different. I'm able to be more focused on being present with him in the immediate moment. We walk along together, holding hands, we talk and we play. He's uninhibited about conveying his immediate wants – 'Grandad, do this' or 'Grandad, come here' – but he knows that not every such request will be complied with in the way he might wish. I like to think of God listening to my prayers in a similar way, and hope that I can be equally honest about what is on my mind, instead of trying to censor my prayer through a filter of what I believe to be worthy and acceptable. I try to work at being my simple, natural self, rather than a projection of the person I wish I was.

That lack of responsibility for my grandson's day-to-day care also helps me to notice how much I am invested in his long-term welfare and flourishing. God willing, I would hope to live long enough to see him reach adulthood. I'm imagining years ahead when we will go to football or cricket games together, as I did with my own grandfather, or simply for walks in the countryside. But the fact that I don't expect to be around on this earth for most of what lies ahead of him beyond that point is teaching me important things about both belonging and letting go. I recognise in my concern for Leo's long-term destiny the same concern that God has for my ultimate end. And in that combination of wanting to be part of his formation yet recognising he will go beyond what I can help him to be, I see something of the way in which God gives each of us free will to choose our path, while longing and yearning for it to be a path along which we will travel safely to eternity.

Somewhere in this, being a grandad has helped me towards a greater acceptance and comfort in my own mortality. It is good enough to be around physically for this first part of his life and to know that the bond of belonging forged between us in these years will not be dissipated by my death. His memories of me, and the influence I have had on his life, will go with him wherever he travels. And when his life in turn is complete, that bond will be strengthened by a greater and more permanent unity between us, one to be enjoyed in the heaven to which God calls us.

Heavenly Father,
we thank you for the memories of those
who were our grandparents
and for the joys that grandparents bring to many lives today.
May old and young ever be united,
in care for one another
and in the knowledge of your love. Amen

Tuesday

Friends

[Jesus said,] 'This is my commandment, that you love one another as I have loved you. No one has greater love than this, to lay down one's life for one's friends. You are my friends if you do what I command you.'

JOHN 15:12–14

One winter's day in my first year at primary school, I made a friend. It all happened very simply: we were playing next to each other on a snow-covered, sloping area of the school playing field; I let her have a go on my slide, and she reciprocated. We're still friends now. We don't see each other that often, maybe once or twice a year, but when we do meet up there's an immediate sense of being at ease in each other's presence. We can talk about both serious and inconsequential stuff or just sit silently; the bond forged over half a century ago holds.

It's really quite remarkable that Jesus refers to his disciples as friends. The term seems to presuppose at least some rough or basic level of equality. If the power difference between two individuals is too great, then no matter what the bonds of affection may be between them, friendship is not the word to describe their relationship. The disciples followed Jesus from place to place, listened to his teaching and witnessed the miracles he performed. More than anyone else they would have been aware that he possessed a power and an authority far beyond anything they were capable of themselves, even if as yet they had not grasped the fact that this was God's own Son who was calling them friends.

What made the language of friendship possible was, I'm sure, the incredible humility of Jesus. Paul puts it beautifully when he speaks of the Christ who did not cling to equality with God, but emptied himself (Philippians 2:6–7). And Christians down the generations have found it to be true. 'What a friend we have in Jesus' remains one of the most well-known hymns of former times. Jesus sets aside his superiority and genuinely places himself alongside those who seek to approach him.

Being with Jesus as a friend did not come naturally to me for many years. I've had to work on it quite hard, both in my daily prayer life and on my annual retreats. Following the advice of Ignatius, the founder of the Jesuit movement, I have learned to put myself into the stories from the gospels and experience how it feels to be with the disciples and Jesus. Slowly, I have become able to see him through the eyes of his first companions and to call him friend.

It has been a transforming experience. I'm now able to sense Jesus by my side, present in the same quiet and relaxed way as I am with my own long-standing friends. I can speak with him, listen for his words to me or simply feel the warmth of his closeness and know that no words are necessary. I can also build on my experience of human friendship in order to better understand just how amazing it is that Christ calls me friend.

Not all friendships last. In my years as a vicar I worked in and around the Yorkshire coalfield. It was around the time of the long miners' strike of 1984–85. I had expected to hear stories of friendships breaking down over one person returning to work while the other stayed on strike. I did hear those stories, but I also discovered those who had fallen out over earlier industrial disputes, a decade or more previously, and whose friendship had never recovered. And that's where my friendship with Jesus differs. I have absolute confidence that he will never betray or desert me. Should I choose to fall out with him, he will still always be there. He will stand ready to receive me at any time, and even come after me, to offer his invitation to make up and be friends, again and again.

My most long-standing friends have seen me through many stages of my life. The person they call friend now both is and is not the 'me' that they first befriended at school or university. And they, too, have changed in more ways than simply growing older. A good friendship is one that can survive those changes intact. Yet all friendships face the ultimate separation of death. How in heaven we will relate to those we have known and called friends on earth remains a mystery to me. And yet I know that my friendship with Christ is for eternity. The one with whom I belong in friendship in this life is the one I will see face-to-face and be with for eternity. And that's a friendship well worth my nurturing here and now.

Lord Jesus,
we thank you for calling us friends.
Help us to grow into
the fullness of friendship with you.
And may that friendship make us better friends
with those we love on earth. Amen

Wednesday

Family

Then Joseph could no longer control himself before all those who stood by him, and he cried out, 'Send everyone away from me.' So no one stayed with him when Joseph made himself known to his brothers. And he wept so loudly that the Egyptians heard it, and the household of Pharaoh heard it. Joseph said to his brothers, 'I am Joseph. Is my father still alive?' But his brothers could not answer him, so dismayed were they at his presence. Then Joseph said to his brothers, 'Come closer to me.' And they came closer. He said, 'I am your brother Joseph, whom you sold into Egypt. And now do not be distressed, or angry with yourselves, because you sold me here; for God sent me before you to preserve life.'

GENESIS 45:1–5

I was born three-and-a-half years before my brother. We were the only two children in a family that was not especially well-off, and I remember clearly that a lot of the clothes he wore were ones that I had grown out of. I suspect this heightened his need to identify himself as a separate person. So, while I followed one football team, he supported their fiercest rivals. It was the same with cricket, though here he did have the excuse that between our respective births our family had moved a mile east, taking us out of Lancashire and into Yorkshire.

Growing up, we continued to tread separate paths. We both did very well in maths at school, but whereas I stayed on to study the subject at university, he left at 16 to begin a career in banking. And when as a young man I joined the Labour Party, I wasn't surprised to find him standing for election as a Conservative. Yet our very differences illustrate that we had far more in common than simply some hand-me-down jumpers and T-shirts. We both grew up being mathematically minded, enjoying sports and thinking that the well-being of our local communities mattered enough for us to want to take part in their politics.

The story of Joseph and his brothers is perhaps the most famous example of what nowadays is referred to as sibling rivalry. Joseph as a young man was clearly full of himself. When his brothers sold him into slavery and told his father he was dead, they were relieved to have seen the last of this arrogant young man. Yet, in a story that presages the gospels, the one whom they have sought to destroy will return as their salvation. Today's Bible passage comes from the moment when, many years after their betrayal, Joseph reveals himself to them. By now he is a very different character. After years of slavery, false accusations leading to imprisonment and finally service in Pharaoh's court, his old arrogance has faded. Beneath it the love that still binds him to his family shines through. Unable to contain his emotions, he weeps as he reveals his true identity to his brothers.

Family mattered hugely in the world of Jacob and Joseph. Indeed, one of the principal reasons for the story being told in such detail in the Bible is that it explains the close kinship between the twelve tribes of Israel, and hence why they should live together harmoniously in the land God has promised them. Whatever may seek to divide them, they remain brothers. The story is told in such a way that even those for whom family life has been difficult, even destructive, can glimpse both what we are warned of and what we are called to.

Rivalries within the Christian community are, sadly, all too common. Often it's the closest relationships that are most prone to them. In my time as a vicar and more recently as a bishop, I have had to learn how to enable people to develop their skills without being drawn into jealousy and envy of the achievements of others. I've also seen examples of how bad the damage can be when a personal rivalry within a church, which may begin with a fall-out over the smallest of matters, grows into a crippling animosity. And I've found exactly the same problems in the charities and other organisations where I have worked and volunteered. Good people, all wanting the best, can nevertheless let personal rivalry destroy the very things they are working for.

Nor am I immune myself. When I hear of some particular success of a colleague or friend, I can sometimes sense the twinges of jealousy within me. I need to notice them, accept them for what they are and then move beyond them to rejoice with my sister or brother at their success. At other times I need to take a deliberate step back from some task that I enjoy, to allow space for someone to grow in their ministry, even when I want to do the thing, and get the credit for doing it, myself.

Looking back on my childhood, I can see how, despite the superficial differences and rivalries between my brother and me, when it came to things that really mattered we stuck together. When one was under threat, the other offered support. When one of us achieved something significant in our lives, the other was there to be glad with them. Unlike with friendships, we didn't choose each other, but we accepted that we belonged together, and lived within that bond, as we continue to do in adult life.

Heavenly Father,
we thank you for the bonds that bind us together,
both in our given families and in the family of your church.
Help us to overcome rivalries,
especially those that lie deep in our own hearts,
and grant us wisdom to dissipate the jealousies in others,
for Jesus' sake. Amen

Thursday

One special other

The rib that the Lord God had taken from the man he made into a woman and brought her to the man. Then the man said, 'This at last is bone of my bones and flesh of my flesh; this one shall be called Woman, for out of Man this one was taken.' Therefore a man leaves his father and his mother and clings to his wife, and they become one flesh.

GENESIS 2:22–24

One of the principal challenges we face with the Bible is to determine whether a particular passage is being descriptive or prescriptive. Is it telling us what we should do or simply describing things as they happen to be? Perhaps the best-known historical example of Christians getting that wrong is the attempts to justify slavery. The keeping of slaves was never set out in scripture as a good thing in itself; rather, a world in which slavery was endemic provided the background to much of the narrative of the story of God and Israel. There's a huge and entirely unjustified theological jump between noting that the Bible does not make an explicit and universal condemnation of slavery and claiming that in consequence it is a state that God supports and encourages in all times and places.

I find that distinction particularly helpful when reflecting on the biblical texts around marriage. How much of what we read is God's abiding guidance or command to us regarding our most intimate relationships, and how much is a description of how marriage worked in the context and mores of particular times and places? Polygamy is a good example of the latter. Few Christians today would support it in other than very exceptional circumstances, yet the kings of Israel chalked up scores of wives and concubines with apparent divine approval. Even where marriage was monogamous, the accepted background was that of a woman ceasing to be part of her father's possessions and becoming the property of her husband, a view that persisted in British law until the second half of the 19th century.

Yet this description of proprietorial belonging as being the heart of marriage is in constant tension in scripture with the imagery of two people becoming 'one flesh'. My flesh is not my 'possession'; it's part of my very self. Moreover, scripture speaks powerfully of the partnership of husband and wife in love. The imagery is so strong that it culminates in the book of Revelation with the description of the church as Christ's own bride.

My wife and I married in 1980. I had just turned 23, and Sue was about six months younger. By present standards that's young, but back then it was very common for those who had met at university to marry within a year or two of graduation. My call to marriage and my call to ordination arose in the same short period of time, and it was always clear to me that without the first I would never be able to cope with the demands of the second. Over the subsequent decades both of us have grown, developed and changed, but the abiding presence and closeness of this one special other remains a keystone for my life. There is a belonging together in the love-centred, exclusive, faithful bond of marriage that not only strengthens the couple involved but also spills over to benefit the society of which they are a part.

None of this is to pretend that marriage is easy. When I was vicar of a picturesque 18th-century village church, which hosted many wedding services, I used to point out to the guests that it took an enormous amount of money and effort, year in and year out, to keep it looking as though it had hardly been touched or altered in over 200 years. And despite the best efforts and most sincere intentions, in a society with high life expectancy, it is not surprising that a sizeable proportion of marriages fail to go the distance. In fact, I'm encouraged that many who have been through the process of separation and divorce seek to have another go. They still want to make the effort and take the risk of trying to find a person with whom they can live in this high degree of intimacy, and do so for many years to come.

And from the massive wedding parties we read about in the New Testament to the complex and expensive celebrations that surround many couples' big day today, it matters hugely that marriage remains a public ceremony. Our wedding day should be open to as many as possible of the friends and relations we will be looking to for support in married life. We need their backing and their avoidance of infringing our relationship if we are to make a marriage long-lasting. We need their commitment to help us belong with one another in the uniquely close way that marriage requires. I rejoice, too, that the church continues to be the place where many couples wish to come to celebrate their marriages, even if they are not regular Sunday attendees. God's blessing really matters.

When I write about the special belonging between two people made possible by marriage, as I have done here, it inevitably makes me think of those who find talk of marriage hard. We have a duty to care for those who have lost a partner, through death or divorce; to be on hand to help friends whose marriage is going through difficult times; and to be sensitive to those who yearn for the closeness of marriage but have not been able to find the right person to wed. We need also to include in our thoughts and prayers all who do have that special other person but where the formal ties of marriage are not possible.

Father,
we thank you for those who are bound together in love.
Help us always to respect and support
the special ties between couples,
who are committed to lifelong love of each other.
Look kindly on those who have no such partner,
and grant that we may find our own closest relationships
a source of strength for serving you. Amen

Friday

People at work

Miners put an end to darkness, and search out to the farthest bound the ore in gloom and deep darkness. They open shafts in a valley away from human habitation; they are forgotten by travellers, they sway suspended, remote from people. As for the earth, out of it comes bread; but underneath it is turned up as by fire. Its stones are the place of sapphires, and its dust contains gold.

JOB 28:3–6

For five years in the late 1980s I served as both a parish priest and an industrial chaplain. With a working coal mine in the patch, I used to joke that I got closer to hell than any other clergy person in the Church of England. It was certainly pretty warm half a mile underground.

The passage I've chosen for today is one that I used often, especially when taking the funerals of men who had worked all their adult lives underground. While its purpose is to compare the search for precious stones or minerals with the challenge of finding wisdom, along the way it provides a fascinating account of how human beings first explored beneath the surface of the earth, well over 2,000 years ago. God's greatness may hugely exceed human achievement, but that does not mean the latter is unimportant. Moreover, the passage shows how reflecting on the nature of daily work can provide insights into the ways of God himself. Whoever first penned the passage had clearly spent time underground – and probably far more time than I did in my five years as pit chaplain.

From time to time, as part of my ongoing training, I would join a chaplain in another workplace. It was a chance to learn from those who were far more experienced than me. Once, in a huge steelworks, I was introduced to a man who was a lay preacher in another denomination. He was on his lunch break and was busy preparing his sermon for Sunday. I asked what I thought was the most obvious of questions, how his working life impacted on his preaching. The reply both startled and shocked me. He was adamant that there was no overlap between the two; his life in his church and his life in the workplace were kept entirely separate. We left the conversation at that, as there didn't seem to be anything else to say. But the memory remains strongly with me over 30 years later.

I was shocked, because it seemed obvious to me that faith in Jesus Christ should impact on every part of our lives. And while I would have understood that making those links might be hard for somebody at a fairly early stage of their faith journey, it floored me to imagine an authorised preacher unable to make any connection. I went away more convinced than ever that I had to work to help people build bridges between faith and working life.

I don't pretend that being a Christian in a secular job is easy. I've known people who have felt they had to change profession because their faith prevented them from doing things that their employer demanded. But I've known many others who have been wonderful examples of what it means to belong with Jesus Christ in their daily work. For some it is the choice of work itself that exemplifies their vocation. For others it is the opportunities afforded to be a friend in need to their colleagues.

When I became involved in the housing association movement, I committed myself to always wearing my clerical collar and using my 'Revd' title at seminars and conferences. I was often approached by people who wanted to talk about how their Christian faith had led to them following their career. Some felt diffident about letting colleagues know this. All seemed to appreciate that my visible presence was helping them to reflect on the links between faith and work and to reaffirm their sense of calling. I admired their abilities to live out a Christian calling, caring for those in need, challenging injustices and building the common good, from within their organisations, many of which had to be faith neutral.

I remember also a member of my church council who told me how she was repeatedly teased at work because of her faith, accused of being a 'Bible basher'. And yet she was the one to whom the selfsame colleagues would turn for a sympathetic ear or a word of wisdom when they were going through a difficult time at home or work. She could have done without the ribbing, but it was a price worth paying for being known as a Christian and hence able to be that helping hand or listening ear.

As Christians, we don't just belong with God when we are in church or at home with our loved ones. We are equally his when we are at work, responding to both the practical and human demands of our labours. We don't need to be explicitly conscious of that at every moment of the day, but we can look out for the opportunities to make the connections. We do so for our own benefit, for the benefit of those who work alongside us and for the well-being of those whom our organisation exists to serve.

Lord Jesus Christ,
whose earthly father laboured as a carpenter,
we thank you for relationships at work.
May Christians always be a blessing
to those alongside whom they labour,
and may all workers find meaning and purpose in their tasks.
Amen

Saturday

The departed

And I saw the dead, great and small, standing before the throne, and books were opened. Also another book was opened, the book of life. And the dead were judged according to their works, as recorded in the books.
REVELATION 20:12

In the mid 1990s it became more common for churches to hold special services to which the relatives of those whose funerals had taken place recently were particularly invited. One of the two churches I had responsibility for at that time had a regular service at 3.30 pm on Sundays, and it seemed as though that would be a suitable time at which to have our first attempt. The event was well attended and went pretty much according to plan.

After the service was over, we offered attendees a glass of wine or juice, and what surprised me was how many of them took their drinks out into the churchyard and consumed them while chatting around their family graves. It made me aware of how strong their ongoing relationships remained with those who had died and of how vital it was for them to have a particular place where they could come and feel close to those they still loved. The role of the church, in helping to facilitate and celebrate that, was much appreciated.

Some years later, one of my colleagues wrote her PhD thesis on the impact of World War I on spiritualist beliefs and what effect these beliefs had had on the mainstream practice and theology of the Church of England. It was a fascinating read, central to which was the difficulty many families found in having lost sons, brothers and husbands whose graves, if even known, were far away in places they had little chance of visiting. Attempts to contact the dead directly were motivated by the lack of other rituals or places through which they could experience and express a closeness that had been ripped away from them by the calamity of war.

I suspect that the Reformation ancestry of many of our churches has at times made it hard for us to discuss what it means to retain a sense of belonging with those who have died, let alone to think of ways in which we can respond positively to that belonging. Outside of more Catholic circles, many Christian leaders remain uncomfortable about sanctioning anything that could constitute a stepping stone towards praying for those whose eternal destiny is now believed to be final and determined. And yet I do want to remember those who have had a profound impact on my life. I want to reassert my abiding closeness to them and love for them, before God.

Many of these are the people who have helped to make me the person that I am. The grandparents who looked after me as a young child while my parents were working are not only fond memories of long ago but also examples I can look to in my own efforts to be a good grandfather. The memory of my college chaplain, to whom I first disclosed that I felt God calling me to ordained ministry, and who supported me through that time of hopeful exploration, still teaches me how to be a better priest. The elderly couple who sat in the back pew at Evensong throughout the years of my curacy, and whose home was ever a place of warm and loving welcome, continue to inspire me with their example of hospitality. I want to keep alive the flame of my belonging with these and many others, with the expectation that we shall meet again in heaven.

Part of that belonging has to be an abiding desire for their well-being and flourishing that is not negated or dissipated by a doctrinal assurance that they have reached a place of perfection. Unlike some who were bereaved in World War I and turned to spiritualism, I need no direct message from them to confirm that all is well on the 'other side'. I just need to feel that I am continuing to hold them in my prayers, as much as I would if they were alive, in order to keep our relationship strong.

I'm helped in this sense of belonging by a comment made many years ago when I was training for ministry. I was lending a hand in a parish whose vicar and curate had both left in quick succession, and I had taken responsibility for finding priests who could preside at the various weekday Eucharists. One particular dark and wet night, only myself and the college tutor I had recruited to preside turned up. I was embarrassed and deeply apologetic. 'I'm sorry it's just me and you,' I said. 'I think you're forgetting the angels, archangels and the whole company of heaven,' he replied, quoting from the liturgy. That night I had a profound sense of how our sharing of bread and wine was part of an enormous heavenly banquet attended by many invisible to us, including those whose life on earth is over. When I kneel at the altar rail, I am united not simply with fellow members of that gathered congregation (regardless of how many or few) but also with all who have knelt or stood, in that place or any other, over the 2,000 years in which Christians have gathered together to receive Communion.

> *Heavenly Father,*
> *we thank you for those whom we remember,*
> *whose lives on earth are over,*
> *yet in whose footsteps we now seek to follow.*
> *Grant that our steps in turn*
> *may form a path that shows a way to others,*
> *a pathway that leads even to your kingdom. Amen*

Week 3

BELONGING WITH THE SAINTS

I've gained a great deal over the years from the Ignatian pattern of spiritual exercises. Not least, I enjoy placing myself in the context of some passage of scripture and allowing God to guide me to identify with one character in the story. I've played every part from an anonymous spectator to the most well-known of the disciples. As I have done so, their stories have shed light on my story. By following their footsteps, I have often discovered something new about, or been able to take the next step along, my own path.

I've tried to choose, for the six weekdays coming, a range of characters. We will journey from the Old Testament heroes Moses and Elijah, through the New Testament saints Martha of Bethany and Simon Peter, and on to two great heroes of the second millennium, Francis of Assisi and Ignatius Loyola. Each of these people belonged intimately with God. May their belonging assist our own.

Sunday

The woman at the well

Many Samaritans from that city believed in him because of the woman's testimony, 'He told me everything I have ever done.' So when the Samaritans came to him, they asked him to stay with them; and he stayed there for two days. And many more believed because of his word. They said to the woman, 'It is no longer because of what you said that we believe, for we have heard for ourselves, and we know that this is truly the Saviour of the world.'

JOHN 4:39–42

Over this coming week we are going to be looking at how we belong with God through some of the key figures of both scripture and Christian history. As you might expect, I have chosen some fairly well-known and central figures. The cycle of Sunday gospel readings often provides something of a challenge to such carefully drawn-up plans, and today is no exception. The Samaritan woman, whom Jesus met at a well, is never even given a name. We discover a certain amount about her background, not least that she has had five husbands and is now living with a man to whom she isn't married, but neither the text of scripture nor 2,000 years of Christian tradition have sought to bestow a name on her. She is simply a member of a group not considered to be proper Jews and a person with a pretty colourful past to boot.

She has no claim on Jesus' time or attention. By all the standards of the day he should have refused to have anything to do with her. And yet well over half a chapter of John's gospel is devoted to her encounter with Jesus. She is the outsider, the undeserving. Yet not only is she the recipient of his love and attention, but she also becomes the means by which many others from her community are persuaded to come and meet the Christ. John tells us that Jesus stayed in the city for a couple of days and that many who initially believed because of the woman's testimony came to have their own direct personal experiences of Jesus on which to ground their trust in him. Had we been given her name, I suspect the Christian church would have honoured her over the centuries as the first female evangelist.

Yet it is her very ordinariness that attracts me to her story. She is no theologian or teacher, no paragon of virtue, no pillar of the community. The fact that she is out collecting water in the heat of the day suggests that she comes from among the poorest of her city. But she responds. She engages in conversation, even argument, with Jesus. Then she takes back what she has discovered and tells it to her neighbours. She doesn't have to go beyond describing her conversation. All she has to do is not to hide her excitement at what she has found. The rest will follow. And it does.

In my early days as a Christian, I volunteered to take part in a mission at the university where I was studying. A preparation evening was set up for volunteers. Many of the details are now very hazy, but I vividly recall being shocked that I appeared to be given what felt like a script to use. There were things that those we were sought to convert might be expected to ask, and these were the answers we could give them. It's a form of interaction that in more recent times I have come to associate with cold callers trying to persuade us to buy some product or invest in some scheme. It felt very out of place as a way of having a conversation about Jesus. I much prefer the unnamed woman's take on evangelism.

We belong with her when we don't have to pretend we are perfect in order to be advocates for Christ. She doesn't hide her unconventional personal life nor suggest that after a single conversation with Jesus all will be very different in future. What she has discovered is simply his love for her, as she is; it is a love that goes beyond anything she has ever received from any of the half-dozen or more men she has been in relationships with, a love that for the first time in her life promises to satisfy her thirst to be loved – and satisfy it permanently.

And we belong with her when we don't attempt to pressure people into making a specific response to the gospel. We just tell them what we have to say and then let them decide if they want to come and find out more. I doubt she was able to put it into any fancy language at all. But she was able to communicate to her friends and neighbours that this man Jesus had made a real impact on her and was worth going to see for themselves. The rest would be up to him. They would believe or disbelieve in him, not because of her words but because they had now met Christ for themselves.

Lord Jesus,
you know us completely
and love us utterly,
despite our faults and failings.
Thank you for counting us worthy
to know and love you,
and help us to be witnesses of that love
to those we live and work among. Amen

Monday

Moses

Moses said to God, 'If I come to the Israelites and say to them, "The God of your ancestors has sent me to you", and they ask me, "What is his name?" what shall I say to them?' God said to Moses, 'I AM WHO I AM.' He said further, 'Thus you shall say to the Israelites, "I AM has sent me to you."'
EXODUS 3:13–14

It was the summer of 2000, and I was in a period of some personal turmoil. I would be leaving my parish in the middle of the autumn to take up my first post as a bishop. But apart from me, only a handful of people knew. Fortunately, I had a week's retreat booked. I turned up at the house of the Anglican Franciscan sisters in Somerset, explained my circumstances to the nun who was to guide me through the week and was promptly told that my time would be spent focusing on the figure of Moses.

I've carried a love of Moses with me ever since, though not because he was a great leader whom I can hope to, or imagine I could, emulate. What attracts me to him is that he is glaringly aware of how far short he falls of possessing the ability to fulfil the ministry to which God has called him and that through his unwavering trust in God, he steadily grows into the person he needs to be.

It has to be said that he gets off to a pretty poor start. His first attempt at leadership sees him turn to violence, killing an Egyptian. When he next tries to intervene in a dispute, his authority is directly challenged, his lack of bravery exposed, and he ends up running away in fear of his life. Yet this is the man who will, some years later, set up a judicial system and take personal responsibility for the most difficult cases. He's also somewhat reluctant as a speaker. He'd much rather leave the main verbal role to his brother Aaron. Yet Moses will become the one who is prepared to stand in the presence of God and seek, through argument, to change God's mind on behalf of the Hebrews. As one reads the Old Testament account of his life, it is the story of a person who is constantly growing into the fullness to which he is called. So how does it come about?

Perhaps most obviously, Moses spends time with God – from his life-changing encounter with the Lord in the burning bush, to his weeks spent on Mount Sinai, to the hours he spends in the tent of meeting, from which he emerges with his face glowing so brightly that he needs to cover it up. He is not simply an activist leader; he is a man of deep prayer.

Second, Moses is always ready to learn from those who have wisdom to impart and to share responsibility with others whom he trusts. He's not the sort who has to do it all single-handed. Nor does he see the gifts and qualities of others as threatening his position. Aaron, Miriam and Joshua are perhaps the best known of those he invites to share in his responsibilities, but they are not the only ones. Jethro, his father-in-law, is a crucial influence, effectively Moses' mentor. And then there are the unnamed 70 elders, who are allowed to approach the presence of God more closely than the rest of the Israelites, and the judges appointed to deal with the simpler legal cases.

Over my years as a bishop, the story of Moses has repeatedly helped me to remember the importance of immersing myself in prayer and of nurturing and growing the talents of others, not least where they have stronger gifts than me. But I've also learned that the story of Moses isn't just one that is useful to those who are appointed to senior positions in church or society. We can all belong with Moses by seeking to learn from his example.

First, we can be people who spend enough time with God that when we emerge from our prayers and worship, even though our faces may not visibly shine, we are aglow on the inside. I know that when I have drawn close to God, in silence and stillness, or in opening up the pain and desire of my heart to him, I feel different inwardly. I might not notice how it is doing so, but I would bet that such a feeling has an impact on how I treat the people around me, how I handle my daily tasks and even how I feel about myself. And it might not be as invisible as we think. I remember when I first started attending a church again in my late teens, how much I was struck by the looks on the faces of members of the congregation as they returned to their seats after receiving Communion. I hadn't taken part, but I knew that I wanted something of what they were obviously getting from receiving the sacrament.

And second, we can be Moses-like by listening well to others. That's not the same as falling obediently into line behind the vision or teaching of some official leader. It's about opening our eyes and ears to a range of different viewpoints and being prepared to allow ourselves to be challenged and to change our opinions in consequence. If Moses could be convinced by Jethro that there were better ways to administer justice, if even God himself could be swayed by Moses' words, how much more open to the wisdom of others should you and I be?

Heavenly Father,
let today be a day of listening,
both to voices we know and trust already
and also to those who offer us different views
or ways of thinking about familiar things.
Grant that we may discern your voice
in the words of others. Amen

Tuesday

Elijah

[God said to Elijah,] 'Go out and stand on the mountain before the Lord, for the Lord is about to pass by.' Now there was a great wind, so strong that it was splitting mountains and breaking rocks in pieces before the Lord, but the Lord was not in the wind; and after the wind an earthquake, but the Lord was not in the earthquake; and after the earthquake a fire, but the Lord was not in the fire; and after the fire a sound of sheer silence. When Elijah heard it, he wrapped his face in his mantle and went out and stood at the entrance of the cave.

1 KINGS 19:11–13

Once a year I take a retreat. For a week or so, I live on the Welsh coast in a house belonging to the Roman Catholic Jesuit order. Every morning I am given a passage or two from the Bible to reflect upon, then I go up into the hills and mountains to walk and think and pray. My retreat usually comes at a time of year when I've been exceptionally busy for several months. I arrive tired and with all the work I have been engaged in still running through my mind. I leave refreshed, renewed and reinvigorated. Indeed, over the years some of my closest encounters with God have come while I've been staying in Wales.

We pick up the story of Elijah, in the Bible passage I've chosen for today, just after he comes back from what was arguably the greatest victory in his ministry. The prophets of Baal were slaughtered, their god proven powerless. Meanwhile, the God whom Elijah worships showed himself in power and authority. Reading that story for the first time, we might expect the next chapter to be full of how Elijah builds on his success. And yet instead he is fearful, exhausted and ready to die. It's only when he is strengthened by God, through the miraculous provision of hot cakes and fresh water, that he is able to journey deep into the wilderness. Eventually, after 40 days and nights of travelling, he arrives at a cave in the side of the mountain, where he will meet with God.

I see Elijah's journey very much along the lines of a retreat. He withdraws from his normal places of ministry and finds somewhere solitary and distant to focus on his calling and his God. Along the journey he leaves behind his responsibilities and cares, his achievements, his ambitions and his failings. And when he reaches the cave, he is called to leave behind something else – his preconceptions and images of the God he worships and serves. Three times he is presented with an image of great strength: a great wind, a mighty earthquake and a raging fire. But to Elijah's surprise God is not to be found in any of them. Finally, he hears what traditional versions of the Bible have referred to as a 'still small voice' or, in a more modern translation, 'a sound of sheer silence'. Now, he is in the presence of God. He can share how he feels with his Lord and then receive the guidance and instructions he needs for the next phase of his ministry.

The journey into retreat is a necessary part of the process. Elijah would not have been ready to find God in the silence and to hear God's new word to him while he was in the middle of his daily duties. Few of us today would have the wherewithal to spend 40 days travelling to a destination and then probably quite a bit of time on the return trip too. When I first started going to my Welsh retreat I would drive there. It took me around three hours, the second half of which was mostly on the kinds of roads where once you get stuck behind a lorry or tractor you have to settle down to a slow journey. I arrived, if anything, even more exhausted than when I had left home. After a few years I experimented with taking the train. Immediately the travelling became part of the retreat, part of the process of withdrawal. I arrived much more ready to meet God.

More recently still, I have sought to mimic that pattern of withdrawal in my daily prayers. I spend a short time consciously setting aside my concerns and cares, my hopes and fears, and picturing myself in Elijah's cave, waiting. I try to let God come to me in the way that he chooses, not demanding he be as I would wish him to be. And there, again and again, in the stillness and silence, he is present with me. It may be just a fleeting encounter, before my conscious mind crashes in again with the agenda for the day ahead. But it makes a world of difference.

The journey into prayer is as important as the prayer itself. In the middle of the last century, the then-archbishop of Canterbury was asked by a newspaper journalist how long he had spent in prayer that morning. 'About a minute,' he replied. Then, seeing the shocked look on the other's face, he added, 'Of course, it took me the previous 59 to get there.'

Whether it is 59 minutes or 40 days, the journey into the presence of God plays a vital role in our encountering the divine. There is much to let go of which otherwise clouds our vision and our hearing. But, as Elijah found at the mouth of his cave so many centuries ago, the rewards are well worth the effort.

Almighty God,
you appeared to Elijah not in might,
but in a still small voice.
Grant that we, like him,
may find places of quiet and solitude,
in which we can hear your words of love,
as fresh today as in Elijah's time. Amen

Wednesday

Peter

One of the two who heard John speak and followed him was Andrew, Simon Peter's brother. He first found his brother Simon and said to him, 'We have found the Messiah' (which is translated Anointed). He brought Simon to Jesus, who looked at him and said, 'You are Simon son of John. You are to be called Cephas' (which is translated Peter).

JOHN 1:40–42

The New Testament tells us more about Peter than any of the other members of that original band of men and women who travelled the holy land with Jesus. It's enough to give us some real insight into the personality of the man, Simon, to whom Jesus gives this nickname, which translates as 'rock'. I've wondered sometimes if the name Peter was meant ironically, in the same way that Robin Hood's giant companion is known as Little John, because Peter has some qualities that are far from rock-like. Peter is the one who rushes in without thinking. He cuts off the ear of the high priest's servant in the garden of Gethsemane. He promises Jesus that he will never desert him, only to deny he even knows him three times over. He jumps into the water and sinks, more like a physical than a metaphorical rock, when he tries to emulate Jesus in walking across its surface. And yet this is the man whom Jesus describes as the rock on which he will build his church and against which no power of evil shall prevail.

I warm to Peter, because his repeated failures leave him undaunted. He's always ready to pick himself up, dust himself down and start over again. There is a deep commitment to Jesus that nothing, not even his denials before the crucifixion, can loosen. In that sense he is rock-steady at his core. And perhaps I also warm to Peter because

I see some of his characteristics, and his character flaws, in myself. I want to endorse his natural desire to have a go, whether walking on water or healing a sick person. Surely that's far better than being so overcautious that we miss opportunities to do good.

Fifteen hundred years after Peter, God raised up another man to leadership in his church. Martin Luther shared Peter's preparedness to step out into an uncertain future, not least when he nailed a list of his concerns to the door of a prominent church building. Luther wrote a lot, and the recent invention of printing helped carry his words around the world. But my favourite quote attributed to him is the phrase, 'If you must sin, sin boldly.' For me, it strikes the right balance. If something is worth doing, it's worth doing even if I might get it wrong. Too often Christians seem to prefer doing nothing to taking that risk. Early in my time as a bishop, I took to advising churches I was visiting that if, over time, they tried half a dozen new things and more than three of them were successful, it probably meant they were not being imaginative enough. I believe that it is by trying things out that we discover God's will for us, not by staying rooted to the spot until we receive absolute proof of the way forward.

Peter's journey with God is not wrecked by his mistakes, but it is very certainly only made possible by the fact that he is prepared to be bold enough to make them. Peter knows he can take the risk of getting things wrong because he has experienced, in his friend Jesus, the liberating power of true and complete forgiveness. Luther, too, discovered that his salvation was not through the weighing of his merits, a reward somehow due for his good works. He was saved by pure grace; that's what gave him the confidence to blaze the trail of reformation.

You and I may not be operating on anything like the level of Peter or Luther, but the same principles apply. Over the years I've worked with a number of organisations that have had to make their way in a demanding business environment, especially through my work on homelessness. One of the phrases that we have repeatedly turned to in such situations is 'risk appetite'. There are some areas where I've learned to have a very low appetite for risk-taking. But in others, bold new ideas have needed to be found and risks taken, not least because old ways of responding to the problems have ceased to work or to work effectively.

Last, but not least, I've learned to take risks and to experiment with my spiritual life. I've discovered that there are particular postures in which I find it easier to pray than simply sitting in my chair. I've noticed how images and sounds can provide a background to contemplative prayer and that going for a walk in the countryside can bring me really close to God. Sometimes I've set out to try a particular innovation during Lent. It hasn't always worked. Often it has been sufficient to that season. But I can think of several significant changes to how I live my life as a Christian that began as experiments during Lent. If I didn't take risks, I wouldn't have discovered any of these. I'm grateful to Peter, to whom I feel especially close and with whom I belong, when I take such a leap into the unknown.

Lord Jesus Christ,
you chose and named Peter
to be your friend and companion.
May we, as he was, be bold in following you,
always ready to try, to fail and to try again,
that through our deeds
your kingdom may draw closer. Amen

Thursday

Martha

Now as they went on their way, he entered a certain village, where a woman named Martha welcomed him into her home. She had a sister named Mary, who sat at the Lord's feet and listened to what he was saying. But Martha was distracted by her many tasks; so she came to him and asked, 'Lord, do you not care that my sister has left me to do all the work by myself? Tell her then to help me.' But the Lord answered her, 'Martha, Martha, you are worried and distracted by many things; there is need of only one thing. Mary has chosen the better part, which will not be taken away from her.'
LUKE 10:38–42

I have a real soft spot for Martha. She gets a bad press for being so busy with the task of caring for Jesus and his companions that she misses the opportunity to sit at his feet and soak up his wisdom and his presence. Yet there's work to do: people have to be fed; clothes need to be washed and dried. I can picture the scene. A house that is constantly being invaded by people wanting to meet Jesus needs a fair deal of cleaning, and somebody has to do all this work.

I expect that, like me, Martha is always happiest when she is busy doing things she knows how to do and things that matter, especially when through her labours she can put into action her love and care for others. It's a feeling I share when I'm setting up our dining room ahead of entertaining guests, making sure that crockery and cutlery are arranged in the right order. I want my visitors to know that they are welcome and that their comfort and convenience really matter. I even enjoy washing up after such occasions, steadily returning everything to good order and its proper place.

The danger for us Martha-types, and what I presume Jesus is taking his friend to task over, is threefold. First, we can end up running around so much that we miss the central point. Second, we can seek to draw those around us into the same world of busyness. Finally, we can deploy our duties as a defence against the presence of God. What we need to do is to recover our centre, our balance and our confidence in Christ.

For me, it's essential to have a disciplined spiritual life. Both my daily diet and my annual cycle need spaces that I will not allow to be invaded by tasks and duties. I need to build and hold firm to a routine that contains both a pattern of private prayer and a rich round of participation in public worship. What I find in practice, just as many other Christians have down the ages, is that when I set aside time to be with Jesus, I am more effective, and even quicker, at the practical tasks I am seeking to accomplish.

Some of that is because I am calmer when I take time for prayer. When we try to do things in a fraught state, we are far more prone to make mistakes. Then, the job becomes harder and takes longer than is needed. When I have a difficult letter to write or a challenging meeting to attend, if I can do it in a calm state I am far less likely to mess it up. I can imagine Martha, in similar vein, rushing around her kitchen so frantically that she is dropping pots and pans, spilling half-prepared food on the floor and forgetting to include vital ingredients.

But the Christian life of prayer and worship is about something far deeper than being calm and collected in our own selves. It's about spending time in the presence of the living God, because when we do that we are slowly transformed into his likeness. The tasks we undertake, the priorities we give to them and the manner in which we perform them are all different if we are solidly grounded and rooted in a living relationship with Christ. Had Martha paused long enough to spend time with Jesus, the most important practical jobs around the house would still have been done and she would have been in a better place to judge which they were and how to do them in the way that would most show the love and care that she was seeking to embody.

Yet perhaps the greatest spiritual danger for Martha is the final one. Could she be busying herself with her housework because she is frightened of what a real close encounter with Jesus might do to her? Over the years, especially as a bishop, I've seen good, hard-working Christians, lay and ordained, who have hidden behind a multiplicity of tasks. For some, labouring in difficult places, overwork has been a defence against admitting that much of what they have done appears to have ended in failure. It's a very human trait to respond to a lack of success by doing more and more. I can all too easily imagine myself saying to God, 'I may not have achieved the things I thought you wanted me to, but look how hard I've been working. Nobody, not even you, could expect anything more of me.' We know that in the presence of God nothing remains hidden, so we busy ourselves away from him, afraid of his rebuking our failures.

Yet the call of Jesus to us is never for condemnation. He calls us to himself to enfold us in his arms, to assure us that we are deeply loved, entirely forgiven and infinitely precious. Martha won't be blamed for the dinner being late or the washing not as dry as expected. If she can only stop running and abide in the presence of Jesus for a little while, all her worries will be put into perspective. She will have the one thing that is necessary and be able to reassess her duties, not through the lens of her own self-criticism, but as seen through the eyes of her Lord. And everything will be different.

Lord Jesus Christ,
you called your friend Martha
to follow you in love as well as labour.
Shield us from the sin of overwork,
and grant that we may ever find time
to sit at your feet and enjoy your presence. Amen

Friday

Francis of Assisi

Praise the Lord from the earth, you sea monsters and all deeps, fire and hail, snow and frost, stormy wind fulfilling his command! Mountains and all hills, fruit trees and all cedars! Wild animals and all cattle, creeping things and flying birds! Kings of the earth and all peoples, princes and all rulers of the earth! Young men and women alike, old and young together! Let them praise the name of the Lord.

PSALM 148:7–13

Since 1991 I've been a member of the Third Order of the Society of St Francis. We're a mostly Anglican group, who trace our ancestry back to the year 1221. We describe ourselves as a community of men and women who 'follow Jesus after the example of St Francis'. It's a phrase which emphasises that our primary belonging is with God through Christ, not with Francis. Rather, we look to Francis to show us the way to follow Jesus more closely.

We've always been different from most monastic or religious communities: we don't live together in friaries or convents, many of us have careers and responsibilities in wider society and our rule allows us to marry and to have families. We came into being because Francis had to face the challenge of an entire village wanting to join his order. He recognised that it would be wrong for them to desert their work and responsibilities, so he devised a way in which they could belong to his movement while continuing to run their affairs. What we've discovered over the centuries is that not living under a common roof makes it even more important that our belonging with one another pays close attention to the life and example of our founding saint.

Francis is often seen as the patron saint of environmentalist movements. He preached to birds and animals, rescued worms from being trodden on and even tamed a fierce wolf that was besieging a city. Yet his love of creation was far more than sentimentalism. Francis learned to see everything in existence as the creator's handiwork. Like the author of today's psalm, he could see the reflection of the glory of God everywhere he looked.

In response to his example, Franciscans try to live as simply as we can; for example, we take seriously the challenge of climate change. As a reminder that we need to tread as gently as we can on God's earth, I'm one of a number of Third Order members who wear sandals all year round. It's a practice that helps me to think of how close I am to the rest of the created order. Each Franciscan needs to interpret what this means for them in their own way, but we seek the approval of our community leadership that our personal rule sufficiently reflects the spirit of Francis.

For me, that means I don't eat meat, I have a modest wardrobe of clothes, which I tend to wear until they are close to threadbare, and I travel as much as possible by public transport. As well as my own personal discipline, I also have opportunities to influence others, both individuals and wider society, and I try not to let them pass me by. As a bishop, I'm able to encourage local congregations to take up the challenge of seeking to become an eco-church and the diocese to work towards eco-diocese status. Through my national responsibilities, I've also helped lead the strategy of the Church of England's investors to pressure companies to come into line with the Paris Agreement on climate change.

I am one among almost 2,000 members of our order in the UK and Europe, all of us with a similar aim in mind. Beyond that, the worldwide and ecumenical Franciscan family dwarfs my own community. I will never meet the vast majority of my brothers and sisters, and if I did many of them would not be able to converse with me in English. And yet I know they not only share a common aspiration, but that, in our various languages, we are praying the same prayers and seeking the same belonging.

Only a small proportion of Christians are called by God to belong to a religious order, Franciscan or otherwise, but all of us are called to pay due attention to the well-being of the planet around us and its diverse inhabitants. And Francis can assist us in that task. He can help us to see that God's love is not confined to humanity but reaches out to the whole of creation. He can teach us to revere the work of God's hands more fully. He can inspire us to reduce the weight of our footprint on the earth.

Heavenly Father,
let today be a day
when we look with open eyes at the world around us.
Help us to see something that we have never noticed before,
that we can offer to you with thanksgiving,
and guide us to live more gently,
in harmony with the whole of your creation. Amen

Saturday

Ignatius Loyola

How sweet are your words to my taste, sweeter than honey to my mouth! Through your precepts I get understanding; therefore I hate every false way. Your word is a lamp to my feet and a light to my path.

PSALM 119:103–105

The history of the Christian church is littered with the stories of men and women whose lives have taken an unexpected turn. Ignatius Loyola is one of them. The youngest of a family with 13 children, he was attracted to military service and fought in numerous battles, developing gifts of diplomacy and leadership as well as swordsmanship. He seemed destined to continue a successful career in the army until a cannonball hit him in the legs and he sustained serious wounds. His injuries were treated in a hospital run by a religious order, where the only reading material was devotional books. Unable to obtain the books on chivalry that were his more usual fare, he decided to make do with what was available. And his life was turned completely around.

Through reading the stories of the life of Jesus and the Christian saints, Ignatius found his own faith came to life. Alongside this, he developed a method of engaging with scripture that owed something to Francis of Assisi, where the reader is invited to place themselves in the gospel story, alongside, or as one of, the characters depicted. On this foundation Ignatius built a religious order, the Jesuits, and a spiritual technique set out in detail in his spiritual exercises. Many Christians of diverse denominations and backgrounds follow the pattern of those exercises to this day. I use them myself for my annual summer retreat. Again and again, I have found that God is able to guide my own efforts of imagination. Through this form of prayer, he will lead me to some insight that has meaning and importance for me in my daily life, both as an individual Christian and as a person who holds office in the church of Jesus Christ.

On some occasions I find myself in the role of one of the apostles; on others I may be a bystander with whom Jesus engages. Sometimes I am still myself, but Jesus and the events of the story are all around me rather than long ago and far away. I have walked with him through the lanes of Galilee and sat with him at the fireside in the home of Mary, Martha and Lazarus. I've drunk with him from the water brought up from the village well by a Samaritan woman and sat frightened in a boat until he calmed the raging waves. Sometimes I have been a witness to the events of Holy Week. I find that the form of prayer that Ignatius popularised brings me really close to God in Jesus. As well as gaining insight into myself and my responsibilities, I return from retreat with my love for the God who loves me both sustained and strengthened.

The world of the Bible can feel at times to be very different from our own. That strangeness can make the stories it tells seem of less relevance. Sometimes the Christian response has been to disconnect scripture from its setting and try to drag it into our own. We endeavour to apply precepts and directions as though they could simply be read into situations never imagined when they were written. I'm increasingly convinced that the universal authority of the Bible is not because we can immerse it in our 21st-century world – it's far too big to fit! Scripture has abiding authority and power because *we* can immerse ourselves in *it*.

Perhaps it's no coincidence that the Jesuits, powered by Ignatius' spiritual techniques, have often had a difficult relationship with the church in its most institutional form. Those who immerse themselves in the world of the Bible, entering its stories with open eyes, ears and hearts, will from time to time return with new ways of thinking that meet the needs of mission today but also challenge long-held positions and attitudes in Christian thinking and practice. Jesuits have been banned or driven to the margins, yet have constantly come back to play key roles in the continuing formation and renewal of God's church, especially when old ways are no longer fit for purpose.

Such insights are a true gift from God to the church, even if they are not always a gift easily unwrapped and enjoyed. Yet for me the greater gift lies in the way that my own relationship with Jesus Christ is made so much stronger and more real when I spend time with him in one of the stories of his life and work. I've learned to live a life both in a modern industrial city and in the streets and lanes of first-century Palestine. Together he and I journey along, and I for one can trust him to set both our direction and our destination.

Almighty God,
through your servant Ignatius
you have shown us a way to draw closer to you in scripture.
Give us such reverence for your word
and diligence in immersing ourselves in it,
that we may ever be refreshed and renewed by its living waters.
Amen

Week 4

BELONGING HERE AND THERE

For the fourth week of Lent, our journey into belonging takes us to look at the wider communities and society of which we are a part. God sees the big picture, and we are called to see it too. We cannot confine our belonging to a safe and narrow territory made up of only the world of the Bible and our own immediate loved ones. Most of us spend much of our lives working in the wider world, and none of us can escape the responsibilities of citizenship, if we are to be true to our calling.

In the reflections for the weekdays coming we will explore how we belong to the wider church, globally and ecumenically. We will look at how we face challenges around safeguarding, how we are confronted with the world of politics and how we seek to find our place amid its diversity. I cannot promise the journey will be cosy, but I do hope that it will prove richly rewarding.

Sunday

A blind man healed

So for the second time they called the man who had been blind, and they said to him, 'Give glory to God! We know that this man [Jesus] is a sinner.' He answered, 'I do not know whether he is a sinner. One thing I do know, that though I was blind, now I see.'

JOHN 9:24–25

Today's gospel reading, like that of a week ago, takes us into a meeting between Jesus and an unnamed person. This time it's a man who has been born blind, and the account of the meeting and its aftermath takes up the whole of John 9. Once again an individual comes to have faith in Jesus, and others around notice what has happened. The big difference is in the reaction of the wider community. We read last week how the people of the Samaritan city from which the woman at the well had come were led into faith. By contrast, the people who are witness to this week's story, though drawn from among groups central to Jewish society, are sceptical and hostile. Their minds are already made up about Jesus. They are confident that they have nothing to learn from him. They merely want to find some excuse to arrest him. No wonder the man's parents are unwilling to go beyond the bald assertion that their son indeed used to be blind. Meanwhile, the beneficiary of the miracle sticks to a similar tack as the unnamed Samaritan woman. He's willing to describe what happened to him and then leave it at that. Others must be free to draw their own conclusions, whatever such conclusions may be.

We know from the Bible, and beyond, that Israel was a deeply conflicted society at the time of the gospels. The Roman occupation was in full swing, and in some places centurions and others had embedded themselves in society, even becoming respected bene-factors of the synagogues. Meanwhile there were groups seeking to resist and repel these pagan invaders; small-scale uprisings were not uncommon. Within the Jewish faith itself, the Sadducees, who held many of the official leadership positions, were battling with the Pharisees over both religious practice and religious doctrine. We read how each came to Jesus with their own questions and challenges.

In a situation already so complex and conflicted, the last thing any of the sides want is a fresh army coming into the battle who is not guaranteed to be on their side. The movement that has been gathering around Jesus in the first period of his public ministry represents just such a threat. It risks further destabilising things, in just the same way that complex conflicts in today's world can be made worse by the advent and growth of some new faction. By this stage in John's account it is pretty clear that Jesus is not going to ally himself and his followers with any of the existing power groups in Israel. He and his disciples represent a new danger to all.

One of the regular pressures I come under as a bishop is to ally myself with somebody's cause in a conflict. A letter or email arrives, setting out a plausible case for support and seeking such added weight as my name and commitment would bring. I'm far from averse to speaking out on public issues, but I've learnt over time to be wary of signing up to others' campaigns. Very often there is much that I could agree with and would want to support. But then somewhere, usually hidden about two-thirds of the way through, is the bit where I can see myself being pushed to fit somebody else's agenda. I know that if I sign up to the statement it will be this tricky bullet point that heads up the press release and that I find myself having to defend in the face of public scrutiny. I've found that it's far better to craft my own words or to only sign up to a statement I have been fully involved in writing and producing. That way, I have a much better chance of being able to justify the position I am being held to.

Like the man to whom Jesus gave the gift of sight in this story, I speak my own words about those things I know, and I try not to get dragged into others' battles. He refuses to be drawn into the argument about whether Jesus is a sinner, no matter how hard they push him. Rather he keeps going back to the story of his new-found sight. He draws such conclusions as he can safely do from that first-hand knowledge and experience and invites his antagonists to do likewise.

Conflicts, great and small, are going on around us all the time. There is constant pressure to allow ourselves to become uncritical supporters of one side. I have a huge amount of sympathy for politicians at every level, who have to compromise aspects of their own personal preferences in order to band together into political parties large and broad enough to be able to run cities and countries. It's only when they are inside the structures that they have the space to influence others to change policy or position. But for most of us, most of the time, the greater danger is that we lose our integrity by allowing ourselves to be too much led by others. Today's blind man is given his sight. And immediately he sees not only the physical world around him but also the invisible challenges he faces. And he sticks to what he knows to be true.

Lord Jesus Christ,
you healed a man born blind.
Give us both sight and insight,
that we may not find ourselves
tricked into fighting the wrong battles,
but strive ever as your faithful soldiers. Amen

Monday
A global church

Jesus came and said to them, 'All authority in heaven and on earth has been given to me. Go therefore and make disciples of all nations, baptising them in the name of the Father and of the Son and of the Holy Spirit.'
MATTHEW 28:18–19

A few years ago, Archbishop Justin Welby discovered to his surprise that his natural father was not the person he had always assumed. When asked by journalists whether this affected his basic sense of identity, he replied that his primary identity remained, as it had for many years, who he was in Jesus Christ. It was an important and powerful statement, one that made further questioning pointless. His response is one I could immediately identify with, and that was brought home to me powerfully when I visited Uganda in 1982.

Arriving, as a Church of England trainee vicar, in a country that was just beginning the long recovery from the tyrannical regime of Idi Amin, it felt very strange. There were few white people who had stayed on through the bad times, and everywhere we went my wife and I were the cause of much interest. Yet on our first Sunday morning, when we turned up to attend worship in the Anglican cathedral, it was obvious that we belonged to a global family. Even the hymn book and order of service were familiar to us, albeit the singing was undertaken with greater gusto. From that point on I felt I was among my extended household.

Since then I have had the privilege of attending and leading services across many parts of the globe. I have been the guest of fellow bishops and Christian communities, of both my own and other denominations, in South and North America and across Africa, Asia and Europe. It means a great deal to me that our common identity in Christ binds us together despite huge differences of language, culture, history and church tradition. I know that it has also meant a great deal to those I have visited, to be linked to the Christian community in the United Kingdom.

In 2016, I spent most of Holy Week and Easter as a guest of the Diocese of Lahore, in the Church of Pakistan. They are a small minority in a nation that is over 90% Muslim. A couple of weeks before I arrived there had been a suicide bomb attack on one of their churches in a poorer part of the city. When the attacker was unable to force their way into the church compound, they detonated their device just outside, killing several people, including security officers. On Easter morning, three weeks to the day from the attack, I preached in that church to a packed congregation, then met and prayed with each of the families who had lost someone to the bomb. It was one of the most moving occasions of my life. Again and again, I heard how much it mattered to a small church, facing threats and persecutions, that someone had come all the way from Britain to spend time with them face-to-face and to join with them in both public worship and private prayer.

I'm a convinced supporter of international church links. The best are those that are clearly two-way, where both parties can identify key things they are giving and receiving. In these links there is no sense of one party being the grateful recipient of the other's charity. I've made it a rule as bishop to always invite delegates from our overseas links, Anglican and ecumenical, when we have a major conference. Their presence is especially important when we are seeking to take a position on some major aspect of how we live out our faith. We cannot make up our minds without taking time to listen to their wisdom and experience. Moreover, it is also important that they see our thinking and hear our conversations, particularly if we eventually take a decision that may not be in line with their own practice or understanding.

Not all of us will have the same opportunity to visit churches in other parts of the world, but we can all play a part in mutual understanding and shared faith. Church-to-church links and those between individual schools can provide particularly good opportunities for forming and sustaining that wider friendship to which our belonging in Christ calls us. These links tend to be particularly strong where an individual has given up the time to visit, and perhaps even work in, another place for a while. Such human contact is a great blessing. We can also include in our personal giving some charity or venture that supports the overseas church, not just for the practical support such donations provide, but in order to then take time to understand how our money is being spent, and to rejoice at the work it is developing and sustaining.

Heavenly Father,
you have raised up people from every tribe and nation
to be your disciples in this age.
Help us to love one another as brothers and sisters,
whether we live close by or far away,
that the world may see and believe. Amen

Tuesday

A multicultural society

'How is it that we hear, each of us, in our own native language? Parthians, Medes, Elamites, and residents of Mesopotamia, Judea and Cappadocia, Pontus and Asia, Phrygia and Pamphylia, Egypt and the parts of Libya belonging to Cyrene, and visitors from Rome, both Jews and proselytes, Cretans and Arabs – in our own languages we hear them speaking about God's deeds of power.'

ACTS 2:8–11

Today's Bible reading is traditionally one of the most difficult to read aloud in church. The long list of different nationalities, those who were present in Jerusalem at nine o'clock in the morning on the first Pentecost, is not the easiest passage of scripture to get one's tongue around. Yet the very difficulty of reciting it serves as a pointer to the sheer breadth of origins among those who heard the first disciples speaking. It is implausible that the several thousand who, we are told, responded positively to the gospel that day were drawn exclusively from those who happened to live in the holy land. From that very moment of the birth of the Christian church in Jerusalem, its members were drawn from beyond the ethnic Jewish family. When we read of how they met and prayed together in those first few weeks, we need to picture a wide range of skin shades gathered in common witness and praise. It was a multi-ethnic church in a multi-ethnic city. Yet, as we know from the biblical accounts, ethnic tensions were an ever-present reality in the world of the New Testament.

I grew up through the 1960s and 1970s, an era when casual racism was widely visible in every part of British society. Racial stereotyping was one of the staple ingredients of many of the most popular TV comedies. Overt and blatant discrimination took place in the workplace, in seeking to find accommodation to rent and in many social institutions. In 1981, I found myself part of a Church of England parish in which most of the worshippers had come from the West Indies as part of the Windrush generation. Many of them told tales of how they had first gone to worship in the parish where they now lived but had been told firmly that this wasn't 'their church'. Yet these were men and women who had been born and brought up as Anglicans. Their home parishes may even have received financial support from church-based charities in Britain. They had expected a warm welcome as members of the same global family, especially in the mother country of their denomination. What they met in the UK drove some to form their own independent churches and others to lose their faith. The ones who had joined our church were among the most determined and persistent. They became crucial to reviving our inner-city parish, which only a few years earlier had been threatened with closure. Instead we now had a new church building situated at the heart of a thriving centre of outreach.

Times have moved on. Almost every parish I meet with for worship in Manchester Diocese has visible ethnic diversity. I would be shocked if Christians arriving in them from Africa, Asia or the Middle East today received the same cold reception that their predecessors were given a couple of generations ago. Nor do they suffer the indignities of seeing themselves lampooned for popular amusement on mainstream radio and TV. I sincerely believe that present-day Britain is less racist than it was in my youth. We present ourselves as a society in which all can belong, and many of us make efforts to help those least like ourselves to belong more fully.

But that is a long way from saying that racism has been excised from our culture. In parts of my diocese there is a widespread mistrust and resentment of people who have come from other lands and are seen (entirely falsely) as having contributed to the lack of good jobs and decent homes for those whose recent ancestry lies wholly within this island. More visibly, we see a regular spate of far-right organisations protesting against the ethnic diversity that characterises our country. The notion that many who have been born and lived their whole lives in the UK should 'go home', to some far-off place they know little about, persists on the fringes of our political culture, reaching out to infect mainstream policies across all parties.

A few years ago I had a fascinating correspondence with a man who wrote to me to object to a TV interview I had given where I supported the rights of immigrants. He described having grown up in a town surrounded and run by people like himself, but that he now felt in his old age that it had been taken over by an alien culture. His sense of having had his belonging stolen from him was deeply moving. It gave me a far greater empathy for those who find our modern multiracial society challenging, even if it did not change my opinion.

At the heart of the challenge we face as today's church is the call to enable all to belong, while recognising that efforts to help some belong more may lead to another group feeling they belong less. The radical new society of which we read in the first few chapters of Acts, where all were fresh in the faith and held their possessions in common, is an exceptional example of mutual belonging; it was unsurprisingly short-lived.

Heavenly Father,
we thank you for creating men and women in your image,
whatever the colour of our skin.
May we ever offer welcoming arms to our brothers and sisters
who come from backgrounds very different from our own.
May we learn from their wisdom
even while sharing our own,
that all may grow deeper in understanding. Amen

Wednesday

Children

Then [the jailer] brought [Paul and Silas] outside and said, 'Sirs, what must I do to be saved?' They answered, 'Believe on the Lord Jesus, and you will be saved, you and your household.' They spoke the word of the Lord to him and to all who were in his house. At the same hour of the night he took them and washed their wounds; then he and his entire family were baptised without delay.

ACTS 16:30–33

In my years as a parish priest I used this story of the jailer and his family being baptised more than any other passage of scripture. It was my standard Bible reading for the many baptism services at which I officiated. It's a captivating tale in its own right. The account of two Christian missionaries keeping an entire prison awake by leading a round of hymn-singing has an inherent humour, and it is followed by the dramatic bursting of the prisoners' chains and the jailer's fearing for his life. It requires no great knowledge of theology to appreciate it, just a willingness to enjoy a good story. Yet for all the drama in the early part of the story, the punchline is the simple statement at the end, when the jailer believes and he and all his household are baptised. I find it very hard to imagine that many households in New Testament times, especially where the head of the house had a steady and decently remunerated job with accommodation provided, contained not a single child. Moreover, arguments that claim it was taken for granted by Luke that only the adults received baptism always feel to be arguing backwards. They seek to make the natural sense of the scriptures fit some deeply held theological presupposition, which is most often the wrong way round. I recognise that some of my friends would disagree on my interpretation of this passage, but I hope they would accept my main conclusion, that children are very much part of the household of faith. It is a duty of the whole church to ensure that they fully belong.

Over recent decades my own Anglican denomination has produced a number of reports into our ministry among children. One of them was entitled, with deliberate irony, *Children in the Way*. The authors wanted to stress from the outset that while our younger members are, like us older disciples, following the way of Jesus, too often they are seen as an impediment or obstacle. I witnessed that first-hand in one parish where I served. Our work among young families had been blessed, and a good number were coming to church with quite small children in tow. There were complaints from a small number of older congregants that having these little ones in our midst was distracting them from worship.

It was always my policy as a vicar to have one Sunday in every six when I took no part in leading, but simply sat with my family in the congregation. So on the next such occasion, I took time to observe what was going on and to notice when and where I felt distracted by the behaviour of others. I discovered that the natural noises of children did little to put me off. However, the very group who objected to them were among the first to receive Holy Communion, after which they would return to their seats and talk noisily to their neighbours; all this while others were still going forward for the sacrament. That did distract me.

We still have a long way to go in many congregations, if we are to help children to feel that they really do belong in the gathered Christian family. Yet I am impressed by some of the efforts made in recent years. Many more services are now family-friendly, while specific worship activities, such as Messy Church, have spread rapidly and operate in a style that involves old and young alike. Often the most difficult challenge is enabling other members of the church to recognise that these new forms of services are fully valid in themselves and not to be justified by how many of their attendees graduate into coming to the 'real services' that we and our friends think of as proper worship.

Unsurprisingly, some of the most profound acts of Christian worship where many children are present take place not on a Sunday morning in church but at school services. At their best they are led with enthusiasm both by teachers from the school and by clergy and lay members of the Sunday congregation. The challenge is then to ensure, if those children persuade their parents that it might be nice to go along one Sunday, that they are met by something they can recognise as a service where they can belong and where their presence is acknowledged and appreciated. Different churches have found different ways of achieving this, depending on the tradition of the particular place and congregation. There are plenty of ideas available on the internet, as well as from denominational children's officers in dioceses and other organisations.

Father, we hold before you
the ministry of your church among children,
in church and home and school.
Help us always to welcome children in your name,
and support those with responsibility for their upbringing,
that young voices may ever be lifted in your praise. Amen

Thursday

A safer church

'If any of you put a stumbling-block before one of these little ones who believe in me, it would be better for you if a great millstone were hung around your neck and you were thrown into the sea.'
MARK 9:42

Again and again we read of how Jesus reaches out to the most vulnerable. Children are one of the most striking examples. The modern emphasis on each child being protected and cherished, with families and parents exercising a great deal of effort and energy in them, is not universal. In societies with high rates of infant mortality, it could be emotionally exhausting to invest too much of oneself in such a fragile creature. Children mattered more as they survived those first few years and became much more likely to reach adulthood. In today's Bible passage, Jesus challenges the cultural belief of his time that children are of lesser importance, replacing it with one of his most shocking statements of condemnation. Harsh words for those who neglected the well-being of children in his own day, and harsh words for us too, when we fail to protect the youngest and weakest.

Today's reflection is one of the most difficult I have had to write. It's probably equally hard to read. Yet we cannot reflect on how we create places of belonging in our church communities without facing the fact that churches have often failed to protect the young from life-changing abuse. All too often we have failed to spot abusers at work among us, even when the signs should have been plain. In my role as bishop I have had to listen to or read the testimonies of people who were abused in childhood by a church leader or official.

Indeed, there is no level of position or authority within the church above which harm can be guaranteed not to happen; some were victims of a bishop. Their accounts are sickening and harrowing.

Society has only just begun, in recent years, to grasp how permanent the damage done to a child by such behaviour is. Until quite recently, the underlying assumption in Britain was that abuse was most often an unpleasant experience, but one soon forgotten. The fact that many survivors were unable to speak of their suffering for many years simply reinforced the misapprehension that it had had no lasting impact. I suspect that many abusers justified their actions to themselves by believing that little or no harm was done.

While some who were abused in church, amazingly, have held on to a living faith in Jesus, despite the damage they suffered, many have lost all belief in a God who could have stood by while such dreadful things were done to them, not least because the abuse was committed by those who held responsibility for them in Christ's church.

I do believe that there is a better place we can get to, one where the safeguarding of children is seen as something to take pride in doing well in church. We can go a long way by simply ensuring that those working with young people undergo proper and regular checks and are trained and supported for their responsibilities. Good safeguarding requires administrative effort and a willingness among staff and volunteers to set aside the necessary time and commitment, but the outlay is hardly worth comparing with the severity of the harm we can prevent. My hope is that, as well as significantly reducing the risk to children taking part in church activities, we will also become a community more willing and able to hear and act on accounts of abuse in the home environment, where the vast majority of it takes place. I hope too that children will increasingly feel safe to disclose their experiences to safe and trustworthy church workers.

Last, but hardest of all, Christ's forgiveness is for all who repent. We must never be fooled into believing a former abuser is no longer a risk. We must not expose them to situations where they regain access to children any more than we would think it safe to offer a former alcoholic a drink. Yet we need to offer opportunities for convicted offenders, and others who present a realistic risk to children, to worship God as part of his family. They belong too.

Lord Jesus,
you welcomed children into your presence;
we pray today for the safety of children
both within and beyond the home.
We ask you to guide the work of the police and other authorities
in detecting and preventing harm.
And we pray too for all who abuse,
that they might find the courage to confess their crimes
and be kept from temptation hereafter. Amen

Friday

Those in authority

Moses listened to his father-in-law and did all that he had said. Moses chose able men from all Israel and appointed them as heads over the people, as officers over thousands, hundreds, fifties, and tens. And they judged the people at all times; hard cases they brought to Moses, but any minor case they decided themselves.

EXODUS 18:24–26

The Old Testament is the story of a journey of faith. But it is also the story of the people of Israel as they seek to be obedient under God and to fashion their society according to his ways. Today's passage, from the story of Moses, is one of my favourite examples. The system of justice lies at the heart of any ordered society. The Israelites have rightly seen Moses as the one who can best administer that justice in a manner consistent with God's will. Yet the work is too much for any individual. A system has to be set in place, one that leaves Moses with a manageable task, where his unique talents are best deployed, while delegating other matters to properly appointed and gifted officers. For me this is the beginning of the political structure that develops over the next few centuries, as a group of escaped slaves is slowly turned into a nation.

The Old Testament is a book about good and bad political leadership as much as it is about religious practice, something to which prophets such as Amos bear profound witness. A people who identify themselves as belonging with the same God learn that one unavoidable consequence of this is that they belong to each other. They must construct and maintain political structures as well as family ones, structures that reflect and sustain their mutual belonging.

As a young man I toyed with the idea of going to work overseas. Part of the attraction was that I found the consumerist political culture of Britain uncomfortable while being unable to bring myself to simply withdraw into the church and cease to let myself be bothered by it. Going abroad would place me in a context where I might feel no responsibility for secular matters. I could get on with serving God by meeting the spiritual and practical needs of the people wherever I ended up, and I could be free from feeling that the political culture and failings of the society around me were in any way my fault or that I had a duty to try to influence and change them. I wrestled with this temptation and discovered within me a profound sense that I must not desert the place of my birth and upbringing. Rather, I was being called to recognise and engage with the political element in all pastoral ministry and to own my responsibility for helping to shape the society around me. That call has never gone away.

Some of the most profound statements on the relationship between faith and politics come from the global south. A Roman Catholic bishop from South America famously stated, 'When I give the poor some bread, they call me a saint. When I ask why the poor have no bread, they call me a communist.' My lasting inspiration, however, is the Anglican bishop Desmond Tutu from South Africa, who put it like this: 'There comes a time, after you've fished enough bodies out of the river, when you need to take a walk upstream and find out who's pushing them in.'

What I like most about Archbishop Tutu's words is that they put so memorably something I have always sought to do ever since I committed myself to my home country. The work of the Christian disciple, whether lay or ordained, begins with the pastoral. It is when the same situation keeps arising that one needs to address the causes, not merely the consequences. As a young vicar, recently arrived in a parish, I kept hearing stories about bad landlords. After seeking to comfort and support my parishioners, I realised it was time to do more. One practical consequence was the setting up of a housing cooperative.

The journey to get to that point meant meeting and challenging local politicians, influencing central government and being prepared to accept the responsibility of serving on the board of a housing association. Two of my staunchest allies were figures in opposing political parties. I learned a lot about the difference between politics and party politics. I developed a deep respect for those Christians who go into political leadership, a course that necessitates all the complexities of party loyalties. Indeed, I am convinced that most politicians go into that work out of a deep and genuine desire to serve their community. While some are corrupted by the temptations placed in their path, the majority remain true and honourable servants of their fellow citizens.

Over the years I have been involved in many issue-based campaigns, but I continue to see such work as an extension of the pastoral role and never a replacement for it. It is also a work that is inherently missional. In the mid 1980s, the Anglican Communion came up with its famous *Five Marks of Mission*. I've used these as a checklist for what a holistic model of mission looks like on many occasions since. The final three cover meeting the needs of the needy, challenging injustice and caring for the environment. None of these can be accomplished without moving from the purely pastoral response to an engagement with the political.

> *Heavenly Father,*
> *we pray today for all who hold authority:*
> *for judges, councillors, members of Parliament*
> *and those who serve on governing bodies.*
> *May they be faithful to their calling, resist temptation*
> *and work for the common good. Amen*

Saturday

Other faiths

A woman whose little daughter had an unclean spirit immediately heard about [Jesus], and she came and bowed down at his feet. Now the woman was a Gentile, of Syrophoenician origin. She begged him to cast the demon out of her daughter. He said to her, 'Let the children be fed first, for it is not fair to take the children's food and throw it to the dogs.' But she answered him, 'Sir, even the dogs under the table eat the children's crumbs.' Then he said to her, 'For saying that, you may go – the demon has left your daughter.' So she went home, found the child lying on the bed, and the demon gone.

MARK 7:25–30

The tale of the conversation between Jesus and the Syrophoenician woman is probably one of the most challenging in the New Testament. It seems clear that Jesus is forced to examine his own position and that by the end of the conversation he has gained a deeper insight into the scope both of the Father's love and of his own mission.

It's my privilege to live in a multifaith city. For 200 years Manchester has offered a welcome to people from all parts of the globe. They have come, with their skills and talents, their entrepreneurship and arts, their cultures and faiths, to make a home in the city and its surrounds. It was half a century ago that, as a young schoolboy, I discovered that many of my classmates were Jewish. I noticed that they got occasional extra days off for special festivals. I envied the fact that they were allowed to leave slightly early on winter Friday afternoons, in order to be home before sunset, which heralded the sabbath. But by and large they were much the same as any other group of Mancunian children; together, we faced the demands of lessons, homework and exams, while playing and arguing over football. My upbringing gave me the gift of learning to accept people of other faiths without fear, mistrust or suspicion. Our humanity was common and indivisible; people's differences were both fascinating and a source of learning. Today I find in the stories of Jesus and the Gentiles a reminder that I must hold true to those perspectives from my childhood.

Like Jesus, I need to recognise, learn from and speak out about the examples of deep faith and holy living that I see in people of other faiths. Not only is it important to recognise godliness and virtue wherever they may be, but I can also discover how to be a better Christian from their example.

I have learned, from the example of my many Jewish neighbours, that my life needs to contain an element of sabbath. It may not be feasible for me to set aside a day for no labour at all; after all, there is housework to do for which my day off may be the appropriate opportunity. However, I can make every effort to ensure that I resist the temptation to fill a quiet hour or two with some worthy task that ought to wait for a future occasion. I've learned simply to sit and do nothing or to read a book, do a crossword or watch TV, without feeling guilty.

I've learned from the devotion with which my Muslim friends practise the disciplines of Ramadan that I should be more deliberate in my keeping of Lent and Advent as special seasons in the church year. They also remind me of the importance of keeping the rhythms of daily prayer. And I have learned from the hospitality that lies at the heart of most of the major world faiths. I think I've become, through their example, a more generous and frequent host of all manner of social events. I've especially discovered how important a role food and drink play in the welcome and affirmation we give to others.

The requirement to live surrounded by those of other faiths is far from a modern phenomenon. In that respect we are actually closer to the world of Jesus and Paul than we are to some more recent ages. It's a less comfortable world than one in which all our neighbours share our culture, religion and background. But it's a world that gives us more opportunities to learn and grow, as well as to have something of value to offer to our neighbours. None of this has made me any less committed to my faith in Jesus Christ that has been the bedrock of my life for so many years. If anything, engaging with those of other faiths has helped me to understand my own faith better, to practise it more deeply and to be even more committed to its truth and wisdom. I belong more with Jesus because I have recognised how I also belong with my friends of other faiths.

Almighty God,
you have set us in a world of many faiths.
Help us to be generous to those of different creeds,
to learn from their good examples of faith and practice
and to recognise wherever we can
the signs of your presence and your love within them. Amen

Week 5

BELONGING WITH CELEBRATIONS AND FESTIVALS

Some of my interest in how our Christian belonging is supported and enhanced by one-off events came as a bit of a reaction against what I felt was a growing trend among many Christians to play down such occasions and even to look disparagingly at those whose churchgoing is largely confined to them. What I found in my studies was a surprisingly large number of people for whom it was such occasions that provided the strongest foundation for their faith and practice.

Over the coming weekdays we will range from the Christian services associated with rites of passage, through to the role played by weekends away and Christian holidays. We will start by taking a look at Christmas itself, the season when so many feel drawn to churches whose doors they rarely open for the rest of the year. How do such engagements help us belong with God?

Sunday

Lazarus

Martha said to Jesus, 'Lord, if you had been here, my brother would not have died. But even now I know that God will give you whatever you ask of him.' Jesus said to her, 'Your brother will rise again.' Martha said to him, 'I know that he will rise again in the resurrection on the last day.' Jesus said to her, 'I am the resurrection and the life. Those who believe in me, even though they die, will live, and everyone who lives and believes in me will never die.'

JOHN 11:21–26

Over the last few Sundays we've followed the gospel passages set out in the lectionary used by many churches for the principal service of the day. Each has focused around an encounter between Jesus and an individual, one that not only changes the life of the person directly concerned but has implications for those who have read John's gospel down the 20 succeeding centuries. Today we arrive at one of the most powerful stories of all, the raising of Lazarus from the dead. Within the theme of this book, it's an invitation for us to reflect on what it means to belong with a God who has the authority to restore to life one who has been dead for several days.

Unlike the three people Jesus met in our previous Sunday readings, Lazarus is not himself involved in direct conversation with Jesus; the principal protagonist is his sister Martha. She is the one who expresses faith in Jesus and calls on him to do something. Lazarus comes directly into the picture only at the very end, when he emerges from his tomb, still wrapped in his grave clothes.

The text makes clear that this miracle is directly related to the fact that Jesus himself is 'the resurrection and the life'. In raising Lazarus he is anticipating what he will accomplish on behalf of all through his own rising from the dead just a few days later. And yet what Lazarus is raised to is not the resurrection life of eternity; it is to complete his normal earthly life and then die. It's tempting to see this as simply a lesser form of resurrection, and yet I'd want to give it rather more status than that. It is a different raising, a raising that speaks of the life we are called to live in this world, not simply of our hope for eternity.

Followers of Jesus are invited to hold both a hope for heaven and a hope for life on this earth. The two are related but distinct. Here, as well as in the hereafter, Jesus will bring life out of death. Nothing, not even a body that has been dead long enough for Martha to be worried about opening the tomb, lies beyond the grasp of Jesus.

To belong with a God who has that power is something that I find enormously liberating. It assures me that neither the messes I make nor the harm I do to myself and others are beyond the capacity of God to reach. My errors will not ultimately deflect his purposes. Where he judges it necessary and appropriate, he can intervene to correct what I have done wrong. With that assurance, I can live boldly.

Over the centuries, Christians have often divided into those who see the world as largely headed on the pathway to destruction, awaiting God's final judgement to bring it to an end, and those who see the world as where God's kingdom will slowly but continually grow and flourish, until he brings all things to fruition. Often in this, the optimism or pessimism prevalent in Christian circles has done little more than follow the general feeling of the wider society around them. I find the story of Lazarus, as with many of the stories in John's gospel, to be one that moves me towards the more hopeful side of the equation; but it does not do so in a simplistic way.

Bad things happen. Sometimes, as with the Lazarus story itself, where Jesus deliberately delays setting off for Bethany until his friend has died, things will have to get worse before they get better. But it is still worth working and fighting for a better world and doing so in the sincere belief that we can make a lasting difference. We will make that difference, not simply because of the strength of our arms or the cleverness of our brains, but because the power of God will be working with us, reaching into places that are far beyond our own grasp, and bringing out life where our efforts would have failed to dislodge the dead.

Lord Jesus,
you raised Lazarus from the grave.
Raise us up, too,
to the fullness of life on earth
and the hope of life in heaven. Amen

Monday

Christmas

While they were there, the time came for [Mary] to deliver her child. And she gave birth to her firstborn son and wrapped him in bands of cloth, and laid him in a manger, because there was no place for them in the inn.
LUKE 2:6–7

I have a confession to make. For a number of years during my time as a vicar, I really didn't enjoy Christmas very much at all.

A lot of that was down to just how exhausted I would be by the time the day arrived. Not only was there all the leading of worship in the run-up to Christmas Day, but what also drained me was the responsibility for, and time taken in, planning everything. Special liturgies required custom-produced booklets. Schools all wanted chunks of my time and energy. Carol services needed to have readers found for them who would represent the wider community, and all those people needed to be contacted, to be organised and to have their questions answered. Alongside this there were cards to be written and posted, presents to be bought, decorations to be hung, the tree to be set up and adorned, and the ingredients for our various Christmas meals purchased. By the time I had conducted a midnight Eucharist and one or two Christmas morning services, I wanted nothing more than to lie down and sleep for a week. I had little or nothing left to give to the private, family celebrations.

Those years are past. I'm back to enjoying Christmas again much as I did in earlier days. And I've learned to enjoy all those aspects of the season that are less directly associated with the theological message of the season. I even like putting up the huge streams of

Christmas lights with which we deck the entrance hall and staircase of the house. And I delight in hosting Christmas dinners for groups of colleagues in the last week or so of Advent.

There's a regular debate in church circles about whether the secular dimensions of Christmas have completely obscured any religious element of the season. It is often expressed with an implication that those of us for whom the coming of Jesus Christ into the world 2,000 years ago is one of the most important events in history should look on the wider celebrations around us with rank disapproval. I'm not going to defend excess or hedonism, but I do think we should be trying to work more with the grain of the secular celebration of the Christmas season than denigrating it.

I'm particularly impressed by those churches that lay on a Christmas Day lunch for people who would otherwise be eating alone, and by projects such as one, which takes place in a town in my diocese, that aims to provide at least 1,000 Christmas hampers free of charge to the neediest households in the community, regardless of their religious affiliation. These are important ways of expressing that, in God's economy, everyone is welcome and invited to belong.

I take pleasure now in writing and addressing cards, and even in the task of producing a short letter about what our family has been up to in the previous twelve months. I try to hold each person in my heart as I write, remembering an occasion or two that we have shared and praying for their well-being. Putting up the tree and decorations has also become an act of hospitality, making the house more colourful and joyful as an offering to those who will visit us over the season, both colleagues from work and our friends and family. The message behind the lights and decorations is that our visitors matter to us, and our participation in the various inherited and shared Christmas traditions that are part of British culture is a way of expressing our belonging together.

For me all human belonging is a sign and symbol of our primary belonging with God in Christ. The more that we experience the former, the more open we are to the latter. Christmas is an excellent opportunity to encourage and offer that.

None of this is to ignore the pressures that the Christmas season places on many homes. Christmas brings out something of the child in most of us and that can bring with it a childish selfishness and unrealistic expectations of how those around us will pander to our wishes, perhaps in a way that we dimly remember from our earliest Christmases.

I've come to the view that one of the key targets for Christians is to do the secular Christmas well. We can be people who give and receive hospitality, who offer support to the needy and welcome to the lonely. We can enjoy food and drink, parties and even the TV schedules without descending into selfishness. Modelling a good Christmas will help to show others in our communities not only how to do so themselves, but maybe even a glimpse of the fact that we can do this well because our Christmas festivities are underpinned by a firm belonging with Christ that influences, however subconsciously, even our most secular activities.

Heavenly Father,
grant that we who celebrate the festivals of the Christian year
may enjoy them in both their sacred and secular elements,
that others may see and believe. Amen

Tuesday

Rites of passage

After eight days had passed, it was time to circumcise the child; and he was called Jesus, the name given by the angel before he was conceived in the womb.
LUKE 2:21

Midway through my time as a parish priest, the Church of England undertook a major revision of its orders of service for baptisms, weddings and funerals. One of the core principles behind the changes seemed to be that such services should prepare attendees for what they would find at a regular Sunday service. Prayers of penitence and collects were added to the early parts of the services and the whole shape was modelled on the Eucharist. There was little by way of concession to those who might find the complex language, imagery and structure unfamiliar and off-putting. Fortunately, the new rites had the saving grace that much of the material was marked as optional or allowed the officiating minister to use alternative words. We were able to work with what we had been given and turn it into something that was accessible and welcoming, while avoiding becoming banal.

Family rituals really matter. Jesus himself underwent several. And still today large numbers of people come to church for such occasions, seeking God's blessing on them and their loved ones at a significant moment of change or transition in their lives. Yet all too often we serve them poorly, seeing them as a distraction from our mission, ministry and worship rather than an essential part of what we offer both to them and to God.

In the case of infant baptisms, we were advised, quite firmly, that they ought to take place in the main Sunday morning service, so that the friends and relations of the children being brought to the ceremony would be welcomed by and into the regular worshipping congregation. We were strongly discouraged from using the word 'christening' and told that 'baptism', a word hardly ever encountered in wider society, was the only acceptable term. The advice was logical and grounded in a carefully thought-out theology, but it was also both arrogant and impractical.

I'd learned by then that those bringing a child to be christened wanted and expected that to be the focus of the service they were attending. This was a big occasion, not something to be squeezed into a few minutes of an event, the rest of which paid no attention to either their presence or their concerns. They were happy to share their day with other families who had also brought children along and content for members of the regular church congregation to be present, but they were not mere guests at somebody else's show. They wanted to belong, not simply be processed through a ritual.

Nor did the regular worshipping congregation appreciate turning up to find their church full of people they didn't know but who clearly knew each other well. And while the immediate family of the baptism candidates might be tuned in and well behaved, their wider circle of friends and relations had less motivation to sit quietly or join in with those parts of the service that did not concern them directly. Services were often noisy, disrupted and lacking in reverence. Regular churchgoers would stay away if they knew that a baptism was planned; they just didn't feel that they belonged in their church on such occasions.

Nobody wanted it like that. Nobody benefitted. So instead, we offered baptism services at lunchtime or on Sunday afternoons. A small number of the regular congregation would arrange to be present, but the central themes of the worship were the bringing of the candidates before God and the promises, by both their sponsors and the wider church, to play our part in offering them a

Christian upbringing. Not only did the style of worship work much better, but the timing also allowed guests to travel on the day itself and fitted nicely before whatever lunch party or afternoon tea the families had prepared. People felt welcome, as though they really were being invited to belong to their church. It didn't need the whole congregation present. Far better than trying to shoehorn them into a Sunday Eucharist, we invited parents to bring their child to our baby and toddler groups. And, once they reached school-going age, we would be there taking assemblies and classroom activities that would support them in the task of giving their child the Christian foundation for life that they had promised to provide at the baptism.

Rites of passage matter. They can make a world of difference to how those who are not regular churchgoers sustain a sense of Christian identity that underpins their lives. And the church is getting better at that. The word 'christening' is being encouraged again to describe the service during which the baptism takes place. If we are now taking people seriously enough to listen to them and to use the language with which they are comfortable, there's a chance they'll get the message that we really want them to belong.

Almighty God,
we thank you for
those who seek to celebrate life's transitions
in your presence.
May your church ever be a place of welcome
to all who cross its thresholds. Amen

Wednesday

Food and drink

In the second month on the fourteenth day, at twilight, they shall keep [the passover]; they shall eat it with unleavened bread and bitter herbs. They shall leave none of it until morning, nor break a bone of it; according to all the statute for the passover they shall keep it.

NUMBERS 9:11–12

Perhaps the most important change I made when I became a diocesan bishop in 2013 was that henceforth the monthly meeting of the bishop's leadership team should include a proper cooked lunch. I've become more convinced over the years that eating together really makes a difference. We belong with each other more strongly and firmly through that simple and very basic activity.

The notion of the shared meal that forges and sustains the sense of belonging among those present is nothing new. The Jewish Passover, with its elaborate rituals, has been handed down the centuries and plays a key role in setting out how the people of Israel relate both to one another and to God. On a much more frequent basis, Orthodox Jews place a high importance on the Friday evening dinner that begins the sabbath commemoration. And I recall, with some regret for its passing, the importance placed on families gathering together for Sunday lunch that was a feature of my childhood. Ironically, while I was never especially fond of the ubiquitous roast dinner that graced such occasions, the event itself mattered and is missed.

Special occasions do go better with special food. As a family who don't eat meat, we don't do the full turkey thing at Christmas dinner, but it still matters to have roast potatoes, stuffing and a range of vegetables. There are always the obligatory sprouts. My wife eats exactly one, enough to remind herself that she really doesn't like them. And then there's Christmas pudding, Christmas cake and mince pies to follow.

At Easter we always have a very particular cake. Cakes have their own special place in festivities and celebrations, such as wedding cakes that are multi-tiered and elaborately iced. Many of the church functions I attend mark the importance of the occasion by having a cake decorated with a message or picture, commemorating an anniversary, a confirmation or the arrival of a new priest in the parish. When our children were small, it was my job to construct a cake in whatever form the birthday boy or girl demanded. Animals predominated, but I also recall trains and even a snooker table. Sharing in the cake, no matter what other food we may have already consumed, is widely accepted as the right way to finish off such an event.

Perhaps the image of the shared cake is helpful when we think about that core act of the Christian church, which is our gathering together around the Lord's table. Paul pointed out to the Corinthian church that such occasions needed to be a symbol of their unity, not their divisions. It was not an occasion for the wealthy to dine well while the poor went hungry. What mattered was the bread and wine they all shared: that should be the focus and centre point of their worship, from which nothing else must distract or take away. We who have eaten and drunk the same things belong with one another in a deeper way.

I'm glad that my presence at a church is often also a reason for there being a shared meal afterwards. It's good to find excuses to eat and drink together. Some churches have a regular pattern of meals after worship, perhaps every couple of months, while others make sure there is a regular programme of suppers scattered throughout the year.

Yet the challenge on such occasions is to ensure that they genuinely are opportunities to include everyone in the belonging that is generated. It can't be guaranteed. One of my most dismal memories is of accompanying someone to a meal in their church some years ago. We arrived fairly early and sat at an empty table. The table next to ours soon filled up with a large party, who then asked if they could take the remaining chairs away from our table and add them to their own, in order to accommodate more of their friends. It wasn't a question expecting anything other than acquiescence, and they looked both shocked and aggrieved when I asked that the chairs remain where they were, otherwise they were effectively telling my companion and me that we should eat our supper on our own. I can guarantee that they didn't mean it as such, but it felt like a hugely excluding moment. I struggled to enjoy the rest of the evening, and never really felt at home visiting that church again. But it made me more sensitive to how such events are planned and run and to the importance of ensuring that they are not simply a collection of separate cliques who happen to be in the same room, but genuinely a gathering of God's people, who belong both to him and to one another.

Heavenly Father,
your table is ever open to welcome guests.
May we too delight in sharing our food and drink
with friends and strangers alike,
that your children may be known for hospitality. Amen

Thursday

Going away together

On their return the apostles told Jesus all they had done. He took them with him and withdrew privately to a city called Bethsaida.
LUKE 9:10

I love big special events, but I'm not a natural event organiser. It's a role that requires a real head for detail, managing everything from cash flow to dietary requirements and from requests for lifts to disabled access. So in my days as a parish priest I both loved and hated putting on the occasional parish weekend. What I most hated was the logistical nightmare of last-minute changes that individuals or families invariably threw into the pot. Just when it looked like the numbers and transport and costs all matched up, somebody would pull out, ask to come along or tell me some vital bit of information regarding their needs that it hadn't occurred to them to tell me before. By somewhere around mid-afternoon on the preceding Wednesday, I would have made a very clear commitment to myself that this would be the last time I put myself through such an ordeal. Whatever happened while we were away together couldn't possibly be worth what I had been made to endure.

But then the day came, we all arrived at the venue, the programme began and suddenly all the hassle was behind me. By the Sunday afternoon, when we were heading home, I would be right up with the crowd who were wanting to ask how soon we could come again. The weekend always felt worth it.

Jesus himself spent an enormous amount of his time with a small group of close friends and disciples. And he made sure some of that time was spent deliberately apart from the crowds, exploring together the spiritual journey they were on.

There is something quite special about going away together as members of the Christian family in a particular place or parish. We knew each other reliably well from conversations over coffee after Sunday worship, from church social events and from many of us being involved in some sort of midweek fellowship group or church council. But staying together in the same place, eating our meals together and taking part together in worship sessions, learning activities, craft work, dancing and country walks took our belonging together in Christ to a new and deeper level. What Paul writes about the church being the body of Christ felt a lot more recognisable after a weekend away.

There was also something special, too, for me as the priest. In most other aspects of our parish life I would be the one responsible for delivering the main input. On our weekends, that was handed over entirely to the host team at the venue. We would have liaised with them months ahead about the sort of things we wanted to focus on, but once we arrived I could be another participant, alongside my fellow church members. It wasn't about ducking out of my responsibilities; rather it was a case of being able to share in what we all were receiving. It helped us to belong better together that there were such times in our church life when I was free to be first and foremost a member of the church rather than its leader.

Going away as a group that already has a common identity was quite different from simply signing up to a faith-based weekend or holiday away somewhere, because we brought the weekend back with us to the parish. That wasn't without its challenges. There would always be church members who had not been able to join us. We did what we could to subsidise those who hadn't the money to pay their own way, but others had family or work commitments or health issues that restricted them. Some people also just would not have felt ready for that degree of extended immersion in a church-based event. If you're used to an hour and a bit on a Sunday morning, an entire weekend is quite a step up! What we needed to do was to carry the momentum of the weekend forward into the life of the church, while not causing those who had been absent feel left behind, somehow belonging less with the rest of us because they had been unable to share our experience.

I believe that such weekends reflect some of what Jesus was doing when he took his closest disciples away with him to places where they could be alone. The level of bonding that occurs, alongside the knowledge that all have heard and responded to the same words and actions, has a powerful effect in strengthening participants for the future. Invariably there were some members of the group for whom this was a moment when their faith reached a new and much deeper level. Often they were on their first such trip, and perhaps had hovered around the possibility of a greater involvement for some time. But the weekend was the crucial moment.

Not every church is in a position to undertake such an event and, even when they do, not everyone will be able to join in. But that leaves me to ponder what are the ways that each of us, in our various and different circumstances, can undertake some occasional event that models being part of a group engaging in an extended faith-oriented activity together, one that we can take back with us into our everyday church life and as a result of which we find ourselves both closer to those with whom we have undertaken the experience and closer to God.

Heavenly Father,
we thank you for the times when Christians can draw apart
and be with their sisters and brothers.
May such opportunities ever serve to strengthen faith,
to build relationships
and to equip your church for mission. Amen

Friday

Carol services

Praise the Lord! Sing to the Lord a new song, his praise in the assembly of the faithful. Let Israel be glad in its Maker; let the children of Zion rejoice in their King. Let them praise his name with dancing, making melody to him with tambourine and lyre. For the Lord takes pleasure in his people; he adorns the humble with victory. Let the faithful exult in glory; let them sing for joy on their couches. Let the high praises of God be in their throats.

PSALM 149:1–6

I've long been fascinated by the events that bring people to church who otherwise are hardly ever numbered among our worshippers. And, being a mathematician by training, when something fascinates me, I see if I can explore it through surveys and statistics.

One key piece of research I undertook was a survey given to people arriving at my then-cathedral for a Christmas carol service. Almost half the respondents claimed to attend church no more than a handful of times a year. What was it that had attracted them? Unsurprisingly, music played a significant role, as we had an excellent choir. The chance to hear the traditional Christmas lessons read out and to enjoy the interplay of darkness and candlelight also ranked high. But I was deeply impressed at the number who cited the expectation that they would encounter God in the worship. It was a clear call to make sure that we treated their presence with the greatest respect and concern. For many this might be the only occasion in the year when they went anywhere with that particular expectation. We had to do everything we possibly could to fulfil it.

One thing I took away from that research was a much better understanding that occasional churchgoers are not always people with little or no faith. Some are individuals for whom the constraints of getting to a church each Sunday are more than they can overcome. Others are people for whom the very different style and ambience of a carol service reaches them in ways that the typical weekly offering would not. I found they were people attracted to the mystery of faith more than its explanation. They were drawn to encounter God and let that fashion and form them as it would, rather than being told what the Christian life demanded of them.

My research particularly led me to challenge an emerging trend in carol services at that time. Increasing numbers of parishes were moving away from the traditional structure towards something intended to look and feel much more like the regular weekly offering. The rationale was to use the attraction of this special event in order to showcase what the one-off attender would find if they had been sufficiently moved by it to want to start coming to church more often. It was a plausible rationale, but my studies led me to believe that it was misguided. One-off attenders were typically people who already knew what a standard Sunday service looked like, and that wasn't what they wanted or needed. They might turn up once to a new carol service format based on Sunday services, but they wouldn't be fooled a second time.

There are plenty of people in our communities who have a real sense of belonging with God, as part of the Christian faith, but for whom the pattern of weekly public worship drains rather than energises them. They need occasional powerfully moving events that bring them close enough to God to keep them going through the intervening weeks and months. They may never become frequent churchgoers, let alone the next generation of hard-working lay volunteers who sustain the life of the local church week by week, but that doesn't mean their spiritual needs don't matter.

Beyond this, I have discovered how important the distinctive feel of one-off worship events, such as carol services, is to my own spiritual journey. Hymns and carols that take me back through my entire life really matter; I belong with them. When I sing them from memory, I am offering my whole life history back to God. I shudder when someone has messed around with the words, leaving me dependent on my hymn sheet. Good carol services combine one or two recently written sets of tunes and words with the inheritance of centuries. They take us back to medieval times, reminding us that we are one in our belonging with Christ with many generations. I'm very fond of a 'proper' sermon, but I really enjoy the fact that a carol service doesn't usually have one. I don't need a moral message or a doctrinal explanation. Moreover, the sheer power of the Bible passages read out at a carol service, as we are invited into the mystery of the Word made flesh, makes almost any attempt at a sermon banal. I suspect that to those who are not accustomed to hearing sermons, that contrast is even more stark and unhelpful than it is to me.

So I find that I, as well as lots of other people, want to sustain and enhance my belonging with God by taking part in occasional acts of worship that have a very different feel and style to them. They refresh me and challenge me as well as draw me closer to the one I am there to encounter.

Almighty God,
we thank you for the gift of inspiring words and music.
May we, through both our hearing and our singing,
find our hearts raised up to heaven,
where the praises of the angels ever resound. Amen

Saturday

Times of rest and renewal

'Come to me, all you that are weary and are carrying heavy burdens, and I will give you rest. Take my yoke upon you, and learn from me; for I am gentle and humble in heart, and you will find rest for your souls. For my yoke is easy, and my burden is light.'

MATTHEW 11:28–30

For most of the past 30 years or so, my family's annual holiday pattern has included a week in spring or summer at Lee Abbey in north Devon. Despite the name, it's not a traditional monastery. In fact, it was built as a private dwelling, but since the 1940s it has been the home to a community of mostly young Christians, led by a team of chaplains, who provide a holiday centre that can accommodate well over 100 guests at any one time. Over the years it has become a place we are so familiar with that we can settle into the rhythm of the house almost instantly. And because we tend to book for the same week each year, we have often found around a third of our fellow guests are people we have met on previous occasions. Our children made friends that they kept from year to year.

For me as a parish priest and then bishop, one of the attractions of Lee Abbey is that it is a place where we can take part in worship without my having to be responsible for making it happen. And as Lee Abbey has a resident community of around 80 people, the worship has tended to be both of a very high quality and helpfully imaginative. We've learned new songs, enjoyed powerful dramas and celebrated Eucharists in unexpected ways and places. There were always very good activities for the children, and some of the speakers have been among the best I've heard. I found that being immersed in such a high-quality, faith-strengthening experience has sustained me for the rest of the year. Especially when parish life was hard and demanding, it has helped keep me going. And while part of me wished that ordinary church life could be like that all the time, in my heart I knew that this was a holiday and it would always be different.

The weeks at Lee Abbey are quite different from when we took a parish group away for a weekend. There is no expectation of having to bring back anything. The whole event is self-contained; it has simply refreshed and revitalised us for daily life. Our visits have given us pretty much what one would hope and expect to get from any holiday but with a definite spiritual dimension.

I also discovered that what I get from such weeks is far more than the formal Christian activities. There is something relaxing and refreshing about being in a place where Christian belonging is shared by pretty well everyone there. One doesn't have to apologise for or justify one's faith. God is part of the background as well as the foreground. Some weeks we hardly went to any formal sessions; we walked the Devon hills and coastline and came back each evening for supper and conversation with our fellow guests and hosts. I accept the demands of living in a society where the Christian faith is constantly subjected to challenge, attack and even ridicule. And I know that for those who work in secular jobs, the level of hostility or indifference to any mention of God is far greater than anything I have to face myself; after all, anyone who talks to a bishop has an idea that God might come up. So I suspect that many of us would benefit hugely from being able to spend a few days in an environment where the love and reality of God is beyond question.

As well as places that provide such a welcome all year round, there's a regular cycle of spring and summer events that combine holiday and faith together. A few years ago a group of older school pupils from my parish went away with one of my colleagues to Taizé in France. As well as having lots of fun, they had spent a large chunk of their time away engaged in both invigorating worship and deep spiritual exercises. They spoke movingly of how their faith came to life or grew during their time away, and yet they were honest that not all of them were regular churchgoers at home. They didn't feel they belonged at Sunday morning worship in churches where there were very few of their age group and interests. By contrast, they were entirely at home among hundreds of other young Christians, drawn from a wide variety of denominations and from all across Europe and further, by the particular blend of spirituality and worship that the monks of Taizé have developed and grown over the decades. What they received from a week away was sufficient to sustain them as Christians, prayerful and committed, with relatively minimal contact with standard church worship, until the next summer and the next journey south. We are fortunate to have youth workers in my diocese who work hard to maintain contact and put on a series of events through the year to supplement these big holiday activities, but it is the holidaying together that provides the cornerstone of their Christian belonging.

Father, we pray today
for all whose faith in Christ
is sustained or developed by faith-based holidays.
We ask your blessing on those who staff and manage
such venues and locations,
and pray that all who need refreshment may find it. Amen

Holy Week

THE JOURNEY TO THE CROSS AND BEYOND

The events of Holy Week draw us into the heart of the mystery of the Christian faith. I cannot imagine doing anything other than seeking to follow Jesus as closely as possible through the course of these next eight days and to try to belong with him on each step of the journey.

We will accompany him from his entry into Jerusalem to his teaching in the temple, his betrayal, the last supper and his crucifixion, then on to the joys of Easter morning. Here, hallowed places, special events, key people and the regular rituals of faith bring all four aspects of belonging together as we take up our cross and follow him.

Palm Sunday

The Jerusalem crowd

The crowds that went ahead of him and that followed were shouting, 'Hosanna to the Son of David! Blessed is the one who comes in the name of the Lord! Hosanna in the highest heaven!' When he entered Jerusalem, the whole city was in turmoil, asking, 'Who is this?' The crowds were saying, 'This is the prophet Jesus from Nazareth in Galilee.'

MATTHEW 21:9–11

I had just turned 19, and was a keen sports fan, when my uncle suggested we go together to the Headingley Cricket Ground in Leeds to watch the first day of a test match between England and Australia. We parked some distance away and began to walk towards the stadium. We were not alone. From every direction hopeful spectators were coming together, like streams joining up into a mighty river. And everyone shared a common sense of anticipation. It was going to be a great day out, and we were all going to enjoy it together. Over 40 years on from that day, it's that experience of approaching the ground that I remember more than almost any detail of the game itself. I like crowds. I especially like being part of a crowd where I know we have a common purpose with which I can readily identify. It's especially good to be part of a crowd that has gathered for a joyful occasion. I still find the thrill of being part of a big crowd coming together for a sporting event uplifting and memorable.

Today's gospel reading, the entry of Jesus into Jerusalem on a donkey, at the start of what we call Holy Week, is very much such a crowd occasion. I've been at churches where we have endeavoured to act it out, sometimes even to the extent of borrowing a donkey for the day. But I doubt we do more than catch the merest glimpse of what it must have felt like to belong to the crowd in Jerusalem that Sunday morning 2,000 years ago.

Rumours about Jesus, about the things he was saying and doing and what might be his part in God's plan for Israel, must have been rife. Was this the long-expected Messiah? Was Jesus the king to be, who would call on divine assistance to lead them in re-establishing Israel as a proud and independent nation? People in crowds catch the mood from one another. It would only have taken one person to throw a palm branch on to the ground ahead of Jesus' path into the city for many others to follow suit. I cannot read the story without getting a clear sense of the mounting excitement of the people in the city. This could be one of the turning points in the history of their people, and they would be among the privileged witnesses who would take the story home and pass it on to their families and friends – a tale they would be able to enjoy in the retelling for the rest of their lives.

Yet crowds can be extraordinarily fickle in their allegiances. The thousands who gather on a Saturday afternoon to cheer their football team on to victory can soon turn to hurling abuse and threats if they decide that their side is letting them down.

So it proved to be in Holy Week. Many of those who had hailed the approach of Jesus with joy and expectancy must have stood in the crowd that gathered on the morning of the following Friday for the ceremony in which they were allowed to choose a prisoner to be released from their sentence. Jesus had been in the city for five days, and the much-anticipated rebellion had not happened. No supernatural intervention had cast out their oppressors. Instead of freedom for the nation, they were being allowed to nominate just one individual to be released from their chains. Disappointed, let down, perhaps even feeling betrayed by Jesus' failure to fulfil their expectations, they made the safe choice. Barabbas, a known freedom fighter, would offer them a greater hope than this Galilean upstart.

The story of Holy Week serves as a reminder to me that when I belong with a crowd, it can be both for good and for ill. It can help magnify my best impulses and desires, something I enjoy when I am part of a large and moving service in my cathedral. But membership of the crowd can also play on our worst motivations. A crowd can turn ugly, start a riot, attack innocent bystanders or become a mouthpiece for racism.

It doesn't always have to be a physical crowd. The rise of social media has increased the potency of the virtual crowd. A group of people posting comments in a similar vein can rapidly create a sense of belonging, for better or worse, to some huge groups of people with whom we share a common cause. Indeed, some of the very worst and very best of humanity have emerged from cyberspace into the real world.

So let today be a day when, in looking back at the Jerusalem crowd of two millennia ago, we find time to reflect on the place that crowds have played in our lives. Think perhaps of a really positive occasion when being part of a crowd enhanced your joy. Think also of a time when you have allowed yourself to be swayed by your membership of a crowd into something you look back on with sorrow and regret. Pray for those who have responsibility in our society for seeking to control crowd behaviour, helping crowds to enjoy their day out. And remember also those who are victims of the behaviour of crowds, including those bullied on social media.

Heavenly Father,
we thank you for the times when we have felt part
of a mighty movement;
for moments when the presence of many others
has lifted our spirits to you.
We remember also before you all who fear the crowd
or have been its victims,
and pray that you will heal their wounds. Amen

Holy Monday

Opening up the temple

Then Jesus entered the temple and drove out all who were selling and buying in the temple, and he overturned the tables of the money-changers and the seats of those who sold doves. He said to them, 'It is written, "My house shall be called a house of prayer"; but you are making it a den of robbers.' The blind and the lame came to him in the temple, and he cured them.

MATTHEW 21:12–14

Some years ago, a national advertising campaign by churches ahead of Easter featured an image of the face of Jesus in the style of a famous poster of the South American revolutionary leader Che Guevara. Below the picture, the caption read, 'Meek. Mild. As if.' Like most such campaigns it was intended, at least in part, to provoke a reaction, in order to gain greater publicity, and it duly did. Most debate focused on the appropriateness or otherwise of the image used. But the heart of the message of the campaign lay in the words beneath.

Things mattered enough to Jesus for him to get angry, and for him to express his anger not merely in words but in a course of action so violent that it caused the money changers and dealers to flee from the temple. Jesus doesn't often get angry like that. The fact that the Holy Week story contains this apparently uncharacteristic behaviour by him is an unequivocal signal that the temple, and what went on within it, was extraordinarily important to him.

In earlier reflections I have explored something of the importance of place in our faith and belief. For the people of Israel, the temple was the most important place of all. Here was God's dwelling among humanity, the place of his presence above all others. For a thousand years it had been the place where Jews gathered together for the great feasts and festivals, and where the regular cycle of sacrifices and ceremonies took place. In the temple, more obviously than anywhere else, they belonged with God and God belonged with them.

Here it was where Jesus' parents had brought him as a small child, to be greeted by the elderly Simeon and Anna. Here it was where he had lingered at the age of twelve, missing for three days until Mary and Joseph discovered him debating with the wisest of the age. Up until his arrest, Jesus spent time each day of Holy Week teaching in the temple. And it was the temple where the first Christians gathered for prayer in the days after Jesus rose from the dead. Holy places matter, and this particular place was more holy than any other.

The story of Jesus ejecting the traders causes me to reflect on which places would carry such importance to me. Where is it that I find the presence of God made close and real in the way that the Jews found it to be in the temple? What practices or activities going on in such a special place would amount to a desecration of it sufficient for me to respond with anger similar to that shown by Jesus?

The story also challenges me to notice when I might have done things that cause a place to be desecrated for others. The temple authorities had a plausible reason for allowing the trading to go on: it made it easy and convenient for Jewish worshippers to be provided with birds and animals for sacrifice and the proper coins for gifts and offerings. Their worship and their access to God were not being disrupted. Those losing out were the visitors from afar, the Gentiles who had come to pray and who would not be permitted to go further into the holiest parts of the building than this court, which had now been taken over by dealers. The action of the authorities had led to the temple belonging more exclusively to the inner circle of its users and less to the wider population of God's earth.

I deeply believe that our church buildings are too precious for us to allow them to become mere club houses for the initiates. They are not there primarily to serve the most regular and committed. We hold them in our care to serve the wider village, town or city in which the building lies. I warm to the medieval image of the parish church as the place where all the important events and activities of the community take place, from festivals to markets, alongside the rhythm of worship. It's a much richer concept of place than the preaching box of the puritans.

Ironically, that means I am often supporting churches being used for concerts, film shows, theatrical performances and even charity dinners, which at first glance might appear to be the very things that made Jesus angry. And yet the reasons for my support are precisely in order to encourage our sacred places to offer a welcome to those who might otherwise never feel they had a right or reason to enter the building; this is what Jesus wished to restore when he attacked the money changers with whips of cords. Often it is when a person has felt welcome in church for an apparently secular event that they feel they belong there sufficiently to come back again for worship or to pray.

So today's story asks us to think about how we can, without destroying their holiness, open our church doors more widely, so that many might come in and glimpse something not only of our welcome but also of the welcome that God extends to all people of all nations.

Father, we give thanks for the many events
that serve to welcome new people into our church buildings.
Help us to open our doors widely,
and bless the lives of those who glimpse your presence
as visitors to your house. Amen

Holy Tuesday

Judas

Then one of the twelve, who was called Judas Iscariot, went to the chief priests and said, 'What will you give me if I betray him to you?' They paid him thirty pieces of silver. And from that moment he began to look for an opportunity to betray him.

MATTHEW 26:14–16

I've never warmed to the notion that Judas was simply a thief. The idea that he followed Jesus in order to keep the common purse and siphon off donations for his own benefit feels deeply implausible. Would anyone really give up three years of their life and submit themselves to the demands of discipleship for that? And is it really likely that he could have lived among his fellows undetected over such a long period?

I find it much more likely that he became disillusioned, his rift with Jesus coming very late in the day, leaving him feeling that he was the one betrayed. I'm drawn to the depiction of him as one who shared the hope that a leader would rise up to deliver Israel from the yoke of Rome and who followed Jesus as the one he expected to be that man. After all, that's what many in Jerusalem believed was about to happen when Jesus rode into town on a donkey. But it failed to happen. The momentum that was built up on the Sunday, and perhaps carried over into the cleansing of the temple, dissipated over the next few days. It looked like Jesus was backing down from the role Judas wanted him to assume – unless, that is, someone forced his hand.

On that night in Gethsemane, when Judas greeted Jesus with a kiss, I suspect that he was more shocked than anyone when his master accepted arrest, chided Peter for cutting off the servant's ear and allowed himself to be led away. This should have been the moment that compelled Jesus to resist and become the spark for the revolution long awaited. But it wasn't. Judas had failed to understand that the kingdom of Jesus does not belong to this world. He had superimposed his own agenda on Jesus, and it had failed. No wonder his reaction was to go off and take his own life, hardly the response of a mere money-grabber.

As soon as I became interested in Jesus in my teens, I discovered that almost every strange group with outlandish ideas had developed a narrative that explained how Jesus really belonged as one of their own. Much of it was so wacky as to be harmless. Not many are likely to be convinced by the argument that Jesus was a space-travelling alien, for example. But not every appropriation of him is something we can be content to ignore. It is noticeable that some of the most extreme right-wing views expressed in Britain, across Europe and beyond come cloaked with a rationale that they are the defenders of Christianity. In my younger days the enemy would have been the communism espoused by the Soviet Union. Curiously, when the Iron Curtain fell, instead of disappearing, this worldview simply found itself a new enemy in Islam. Jesus does not need such warriors to defend him, any more than he needed an army in Jerusalem.

I can spot these appropriations of Christ most readily in the agendas of those with whom I heartily disagree. I need to be more careful in order to find them woven into causes with which I have sympathy. I have high regard for the words and works of Christian leaders and communities in South America who first gave us what came to be known as liberation theology. I do believe that Jesus wants all people to be free and that we miss the point if we entirely make that a matter for heaven rather than a cause for determined action on earth. But then I need to watch out for signs that I am confining Jesus purely to a political role, one that he expressly rejected when the devil offered it to him on a mountaintop at the start of his ministry.

It's hardest of all when the appropriation takes place within me, when it is my personal agenda that I am requiring Jesus to sign up to as a condition for my following him. I don't want to identify with Judas. I don't wish to believe that I belong with him, among those who betray Jesus. And yet sometimes that is exactly where I fit into the story, because I've done the same as Judas did. I've come to Jesus with my own agenda and tried to force him to fit within it.

I know that I do that, because I am a far-from-perfect human being. While I see such behaviour more readily in others, I know that I cannot be exempt from it myself. The focus for today, then, should perhaps be not on the sins and errors of others but on our own. What are the things I do or believe that amount to imposing my agenda on Jesus? Am I sometimes guilty of saying to him, 'I will follow you but only as long as it is by this particular route or to that specific destination'?

Heavenly Father,
forgive me the times when I have betrayed the trust of others.
Help me to be loyal and trustworthy
and to follow not my own agenda
but where you would have me travel. Amen

Holy Wednesday

Jesus in danger

After a little while the bystanders came up and said to Peter, 'Certainly you are also one of them, for your accent betrays you.' Then he began to curse, and he swore an oath, 'I do not know the man!' At that moment the cock crowed. Then Peter remembered what Jesus had said: 'Before the cock crows, you will deny me three times.' And he went out and wept bitterly.

MATTHEW 26:73–75

Poor Peter. He was one of Jesus' closest companions. He promised his Lord that he would never deny or desert him. And yet, faced with danger, he insisted three times over that he had no knowledge of him. Only when the cock crowed did the light dawn on Peter. Only then did he grasp the tragedy of what he had done.

I've got a fair amount of sympathy for him. I guess Peter hoped that by pretending not to have a connection with the man being questioned, he might be able to stay close and watch what happened. He was trying to keep near to Jesus, not to distance himself from him. He was going for the practical solution in a context where he was in real personal danger. What had just happened to his leader could well be turned on him next. Reading on in the story, we know that it didn't take long after the first Pentecost for Peter to be arrested and locked up. But by then, chastened by his Holy Week experience and buoyed by Easter and the coming of the Holy Spirit, Peter was a different man.

Times of danger can bring out the very worst in us. The collapse of some of the eastern European countries in the 1990s led to people who had lived harmoniously together over many years turning on their neighbours. In lands not all that far from here, and cultures not so different from our own, atrocities were committed that could reasonably be called genocide. Similar things were taking place further afield in Rwanda. Those who had formerly been happy to belong together, notwithstanding ethnic, tribal or religious difference, set themselves at one another's throats.

Yet I have also seen how danger can bring out the best. Over the past few years I have taken part in a number of ceremonies to commemorate the centenaries of acts of valour during World War I that led to the awarding of the Victoria Cross. We have remembered people of extraordinary courage who went beyond the call of duty, often putting themselves into terrible danger, in order to protect the lives of their comrades. Their sense of belonging with their fellow service members, and perhaps also to their nation, overrode their natural human instinct for self-preservation.

I've seen it, too, in other parts of the Anglican Communion, where Christians can face both steady low-level prejudice and occasional serious risk to life and limb. The shared danger of their position becomes one of the forces that bind them together. At the same time, their meditation on the suffering of Christ helps them to know that in what they are undergoing they belong very much with their Lord. I have prayed with those who have lost loved ones to an attack from a suicide bomber. I have been amazed at how joyfully they are able to worship, notwithstanding their recent bereavement, because they know that Jesus is with them in their suffering.

And what I found there I have discovered to be true in my own heart. There have been times in my life that have been difficult and full of threat. I wondered in my earliest years as a Christian whether it was simply the fact that I lived a secure and fairly successful life that allowed me to believe and practise my faith. Would I find all that I believed vanishing in the event of it being put under real pressure? And yet it was precisely when things were at their worst that I found

Christ coming closest. Far from leaving me on my own to face my troubles, he drew nearer than ever before, becoming truly my source of consolation. The story of Holy Week is especially important at such times, because it is a story of triumph over the worst that can be done. Apart from Judas, nobody was lost. The danger, great though it may be, can only affect us in and for this life; it cannot deny us our eternity with God.

We know we will get it wrong. We will hide our allegiance to Christ at work or school, among our family members or when out with friends. When we do so, whether the danger is physical threat or the more likely risk of verbal attack and ridicule, we belong with Peter. But Peter was far from irredeemable. He went on to be the leader of the apostles. Peter began the mission to the Gentiles, laying out the gospel before Cornelius and his companions. Peter took the good news to the very heart of the empire, to Rome itself. Having let his Lord down in the teeth of one particular danger, he faced up to many greater dangers down the years to come. You and I belong with him in this, just as much as we belong with him in his denial.

Lord Jesus,
we thank you that you never desert us in danger.
Be close to those in fear or peril this day,
especially those who suffer for their faith in you.
Grant us courage in the face of attack or ridicule
and bravery when we feel least secure. Amen

Maundy Thursday

Washing the disciples' feet

Then he poured water into a basin and began to wash the disciples' feet and to wipe them with the towel that was tied around him. He came to Simon Peter, who said to him, 'Lord, are you going to wash my feet?' Jesus answered, 'You do not know now what I am doing, but later you will understand.' Peter said to him, 'You will never wash my feet.' Jesus answered, 'Unless I wash you, you have no share with me.'
JOHN 13:5–8

John treats the account of that Thursday night in a unique and amazing way. Earlier chapters of his gospel are so full of eucharistic imagery that he can leave the last supper itself entirely out of his narrative, to make space for the challenging story of Jesus washing his followers' feet. He makes it abundantly clear to Peter that allowing him to wash his feet is an essential component of their belonging together – so much so that, once Peter gets the point, he is clamouring for other parts of his body to be given the same treatment.

It's not surprising that when, after Easter, the disciples began to re-enact the events of that occasion on a weekly basis, it was the breaking of bread and sharing of wine that became the focus, not a foot-washing ceremony. Yet the image was too powerful to die out entirely. Medieval kings performed it annually, in a rite that in Britain has become the Maundy Service – the ritual of the monarch taking up a bowl and towel being replaced by gifts of purses of money, presumably to the mutual satisfaction of all concerned.

More recently, foot washing has emerged as an annual practice in many Anglican churches. And I think it does us good. Being the one who is usually leading the worship, it tends to fall to me to perform the washing. I'm always struck by the sheer variety of feet with which I am presented. Their range of colour and size and the different evidence they bear of the lives of those to whom they are attached speak powerfully of the diversity of God's people. But above all else it serves as a strong reminder that the office I have the privilege of holding is rooted in service.

There is a profound humility in washing the feet of others. Pope Francis expressed that to a degree which offended some more traditionally minded Roman Catholics when, early in his pontificate, he washed the feet not just of carefully chosen priests, as previous popes had done, but of lay men and women and even a Muslim. He put the ritual back where it belonged, making a powerful statement about who Christ came to serve and whom he calls us to serve today.

Because I spend Holy Week somewhere different each year, there is almost always something new and challenging to the experience. Recently, I found that on a particular Maundy Thursday it would not be me washing the feet; instead, I would be among those whose feet were to be washed. To my surprise I found that submitting myself to the physical care of another, to perform something that I could more easily do for myself, was an equally moving and humbling experience, which years of always being the foot washer had deprived me of.

It took me back to an incident soon after I was ordained. I was visiting a house ahead of taking a funeral. The next of kin was clearly struggling to cope but was determined to make me a cup of tea. When the pot brewed, he discovered he had no milk in the house. He looked for powdered milk or even a tin of evaporated milk but found nothing. I assured him that I was happy to drink it black, but that wasn't acceptable to him. From the depths of his kitchen cupboard he emerged with a tin of custard powder, a large spoonful of which he carefully stirred into my drink. It was absolutely foul. But I knew that at this moment my taste buds mattered far less than his dignity. I had to let him serve me, even if I would have much preferred not to. I drank the tea.

I'd largely forgotten that incident, but allowing my feet to be washed in church brought it back. And when I read again the gospel account, I noticed that Jesus did not suggest that future leaders of the church should wash their own feet but that they should perform this service for one another. The mutuality in the action deepens the belonging. I must try to live as one who stands ready to wash and to be washed, to serve and to be served. Moreover, I must be prepared to give service to, and accept it from, not just the obvious but the unlikely.

Lord Jesus,
on the night of your betrayal, you washed your followers' feet.
May we be ever willing both to serve
and to receive the service of others, given in your name. Amen

Good Friday

At the foot of the cross

At three o'clock Jesus cried out with a loud voice, 'Eloi, Eloi, lema sabachthani?' which means, 'My God, my God, why have you forsaken me?' When some of the bystanders heard it, they said, 'Listen, he is calling for Elijah.' And someone ran, filled a sponge with sour wine, put it on a stick, and gave it to him to drink, saying, 'Wait, let us see whether Elijah will come to take him down.' Then Jesus gave a loud cry and breathed his last. And the curtain of the temple was torn in two, from top to bottom. Now when the centurion, who stood facing him, saw that in this way he breathed his last, he said, 'Truly this man was God's Son!'

MARK 15:34–39

Like many clergy, I have a small number of set-piece talks that I can give more or less at the drop of a hat. One of them is a journey through the artworks of the first and second millennia, looking at how the story of Good Friday is depicted. There is a startling contrast between earlier works and those that come from the late medieval period onwards. In art from the first thousand years, there is an entire absence of Jesus' suffering. Where Jesus is shown carrying his cross, it looks far less like an instrument of bloody torture than it resembles the processional crosses carried in and out of many Anglican churches at the start and end of Sunday services. And when he is depicted fastened to the cross, he gazes serenely out at the observer, remaining somehow untouched by what is being done to him.

By around the 15th century all has changed. Now we see Jesus writhing in agony. His body, distorted by pain, is scarred or pockmarked. From the foot of the cross Mary and John, sometimes with others, gaze on the scene in horror. It's a tradition that was already emerging in the early 13th century, when Francis of Assisi took it to the next level by declaring that it was only through feeling the suffering of Christ at his crucifixion that we could hope to grasp the love of us for which he went to the cross. Francis prayed that he might feel both, to the fullest possible extent, in his own body. And he did.

For the earlier period it is the simple fact that the Son of God died on the cross which matters, and at one level I can see that this is so central to our faith that we run risk by adding to it. But we are called not just to be the beneficiaries of some strange transaction by which our gateway to eternity is thrown open; we are called also to a living and intimate relationship with Christ here and now, a relationship that is a foretaste of the life beyond. If I am to truly enter into such a relationship, then, like Francis, I need to engage with the incredible love that is offered to me. I cannot satisfactorily do so unless I confront the moment when that love is most stark and visible. We need to stand by the cross, as those who belong with Jesus in his suffering, as much as we belong with him in the stories of his healings, his miracles and his teaching.

What needs to be remembered in such devotional exercises is that it is the love that is the focus, not the pain and agony in itself. In and around the time of Francis, groups known as flagellants sprang up. Those fellowships indulged in extreme beatings, of either one another or themselves, seemingly in the belief that the pains they bore would help atone for their sins. Such practices were condemned by church authorities at the time, as we would today, not least because they too easily provide the excuse for sexual or other abuse. When we look today at the face of the one suffering on the cross, we need to see that it is love, not nails, that holds him there, a love that flows out from him to you and me. Our calling is to be those who are willing to so bask in the light of that love that it fills us and overflows, until we become filled with a love not only for the one who first loved us but for the whole of the world for which he was willing to suffer.

Down the generations, Christians have discovered that gazing at Christ on the cross is a particular help in times of suffering. For many British troops in World War I, the simple Calvary scenes often found at crossroads in France and Belgium became a powerful aid to coping with the horrors of war. Some of the artworks that emerged then and over the next few years took traditional images of the crucifixion and replaced the figures of Jesus and his companions with images of soldiers dying in no man's land.

I know that I cannot get anywhere close to the prayer that Francis prayed. But I can continue to try, especially each year on Good Friday, to approach that place where love overcomes first suffering and then death. I can stay with my Lord in his agony, as closely as I can bear, for as long as I can bear. And I know that when I do so, I will emerge different.

Heavenly Father,
you saw your Son suffer upon the cross.
May we who also gaze on his Passion this day
be comforted by the immensity of his love,
who died that we might live. Amen

Holy Saturday

A day of puzzlement

They took the body of Jesus and wrapped it with the spices in linen cloths, according to the burial custom of the Jews. Now there was a garden in the place where he was crucified, and in the garden there was a new tomb in which no one had ever been laid. And so, because it was the Jewish day of Preparation, and the tomb was nearby, they laid Jesus there.
JOHN 19:40–42

It didn't take long for the Christian church to notice the gap in the Holy Week timetable. Jesus died on a Friday afternoon. He rose from the dead early on Sunday morning. So what was he up to in between? The answer they found was that his mission, completed on earth, was now being taken through the very gates of hell itself, to bring out of their prison those for whom he had died but whose deaths had preceded his own. I'm fond of a medieval picture that shows him raising Adam and Eve from their tombs, gently holding their hands as they look slightly perplexed by this dramatic turn of events.

The gospels, of course, are silent about what happened over that period, so not all Christians will accept what is traditionally referred to as the harrowing of hell. But it is an incident that raises important questions about just how far the saving power of Jesus reaches. As well as those who have responded to the gospel in this life, does he also reach and save others who died before him? If so, what about those who lived in later years but in lands far from where Christianity spread, people who had no opportunity to hear the good news? And where do those stand who may have heard only a debased or partial version of his message, perhaps filtered through the lens of another religion or distorted by a society bent on materialism?

Some of us will be content with the narrowest of answers, where only those who were supernaturally granted a vision of the future Christ, and responded to it, can be saved. After all, every human being is a sinner, and none merit anything other than hell. When Jesus says, 'Abraham rejoiced that he would see my day; he saw it and was glad' (John 8:56), he might be alluding to one such candidate. But I don't think these are matters we should cease too easily to struggle with, not least because narrow interpretations seem to place God's justice over and above God's love. For me, love must always come top of the list.

It's a question that the great Christian writer C.S. Lewis took up in his book *The Last Battle*, the final and apocalyptic instalment of his 'Chronicles of Narnia'. Towards the very end we read of the death in battle of a fighter in the army that has opposed the lion Aslan (who for Lewis represents Christ). This man has, however, lived a life marked by goodness in all its aspects. What he discovers on his death is that it has not been the god he believed himself to be following that he has truly served, but Aslan himself. It's a theme also taken up by the 20th-century Catholic theologian Karl Rahner, who spoke, in language that today can sound condescending, of 'anonymous Christians', people who follow Christ without realising it.

Today is doubly a good day to reflect on such things. Not only is it the day traditionally associated with this extension of Christ's mission, but it is also a day of emptiness, of not knowing; it is a day of silence, not of clear answers. Today churches are largely barren, except for the preparations for Easter worship. The liturgical provision is sparse. We are encouraged to go out and see the desolation of a world that largely lacks answers. It's a day to imagine what the world might look like if Christ had not come to save it, one when I let myself notice the sheer emptiness of much of the stuff with which human beings fill their lives: the blind chasing after material goods that can never satisfy; the weight placed on relationships that are destined to let us down; the pursuit of power that will always be lost in death. And yet this is the world for which Jesus died.

Today we can quietly puzzle over mysteries for which we will not receive an answer. In doing so, we will be making the best preparation we can for the greatest mystery of all, the one that we shall be united in celebrating with Christians from all sorts of backgrounds, traditions, beliefs and denominations, tomorrow.

Almighty God,
we thank you for the great mysteries of faith.
Help us not to be afraid
of things for which there are no simple answers,
but to abide with you, until the light dawns from above. Amen

Easter Day

Alleluia!

Jesus said to her, 'Mary!' She turned and said to him in Hebrew, 'Rabbouni!' (which means Teacher). Jesus said to her, 'Do not hold on to me, because I have not yet ascended to the Father. But go to my brothers and say to them, "I am ascending to my Father and your Father, to my God and your God."' Mary Magdalene went and announced to the disciples, 'I have seen the Lord'; and she told them that he had said these things to her.

JOHN 20:16–18

Today is the day we celebrate. Our Lenten fast and discipline are over. Today we belong with a risen Jesus. Death has failed to maintain its grip on him. Alive in Jerusalem 2,000 years ago, he remains alive everywhere and ever since.

I love the fact that, while the body of Jesus is somehow different after Easter, it retains the marks of the nails in his hands and his feet and of the spear in his side. He is still the one who has come through suffering and death, and yet he has broken every barrier and boundary.

I am fond of a maxim someone told me a few years ago: 'God draws, but the devil drives.' It's an image that fits well with the biblical image of the shepherd who walks ahead of his flock, calling them to follow him rather than remaining at their rear and sending dogs to chivvy them along. It also makes the point that God is one who attracts us rather than drives us on. There is also something deeply unhealthy about being the sort of person who can be described as 'driven', even if they appear to be enormously successful. The Easter stories are full of the Jesus who draws instead of drives. He goes ahead of them into Galilee, calling them to meet with him if they will. In the final chapter of John's gospel, we find Jesus at the lakeside, preparing a fire on which breakfast can be cooked and calling Peter and his companions across the water to come and join him.

I think we can use that distinction between drawing and driving as a method of discernment, to help us work out whether a particular direction for our lives is of God or not. Is what lies before us something that attracts us spiritually, in the deepest part of our selves, or do we feel driven and compelled to travel that path by other forces?

There is also a powerful sense of movement and dynamism in the risen Jesus who draws. He meets with his friends and then quickly moves on to the next place of rendezvous. Being drawn by him is not a single event but a lifelong process. Indeed, it's a process that goes beyond this lifetime. We who are drawn to follow Jesus on earth are drawn to join him in heaven. The more we have accustomed ourselves to hearing and following his voice here, the readier we will be for eternity.

Images of the risen Jesus in art have tried to capture this sense of the one who draws us towards him but will never be within our grasp. Perhaps the most effective and the best known is by Titian. In it we see the scene related to us by John in today's passage: Jesus and Mary Magdalene on Easter morning, meeting in the garden. She is on her knees straining towards him. He stands before her in an attitude that, while offering blessing and protection, makes it plain that she may not touch him. All around him the brown of the earth is turning green with new life, while a tree above breaks into leaf. Jesus is both with Mary, restored to her, and yet beyond her.

Not only is it a magnificent painting, but it has a moving story attached to it. It forms part of the permanent collection of the National Gallery in London, from which all the valuable works of art were evacuated during World War II. The authorities of the Gallery looked at their empty walls, felt a symbolic gesture needed to be made and decided that one work of art should be brought back each month as a sign of life going on. A poll was held to determine which picture the people most wanted to see. It was Titian's work that won. This was the image that would most sustain the people of Britain in the darkest time of war. This was what portrayed hope and purpose and resurrection.

Mary and Jesus belong with each other. She will continue to follow his call on earth and knows that she will be united with him in heaven. The words unspoken by both Mary and Jesus in Titian's picture, yet which I believe to be underpinning all that he portrays, are the title I have given this little collection of Lenten reflections: you are mine.

Lord Jesus Christ,
we thank you for the completion of our Lenten disciplines.
Grant us this day the same joy in your resurrection that Mary knew,
and may we, like her, belong forever with you. Amen

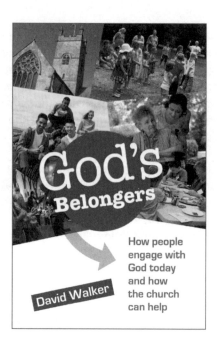

'Once in a while, a book comes along that changes the way you look at things… David Walker's delightfully titled *God's Belongers* analyses the different ways in which people express their belonging to church and their engagement with God, and suggests new strategies that will help the local church understand and provide for this belonging.'
Rt Revd Stephen Cottrell, Bishop of Chelmsford

'This book encourages us to look seriously at those not like us so that we can welcome them. It also challenges us to learn from others.'
Elizabeth Clark, National Rural Officer for the Methodist and United Reformed Churches

God's Belongers
How people engage with God today and how the church can help
David Walker
978 0 85746 467 5 £7.99

brfonline.org.uk